Pupil Book

5

Heinemann

Series editors	Peter Clarke
	Len Frobisher
Writing team	Janine Blinko
	Paula Coombes
	Hilary Koll
	Steve Mills
	Jeanette Mumford

Heinemann Educational Publishers
Halley Court, Jordan Hill, Oxford, OX2 8EJ
a division of Harcourt Education Ltd
www.heinemann.co.uk

Heinemann is a registered trademark of Harcourt Education Ltd

First published 2003

06 05 04 03
10, 9, 8, 7, 6, 5, 4, 3, 2, 1

ISBN 0 435 20722 9

Illustrated by Andy Hammond
Cover illustration by Dave Cockburn
Cover design by Paul Goodman
Designed by bigtop, Bicester, UK
Printed in Spain by Edelvives

Contents

Let's practise

1 Multiply each number by 10.
What happens to each digit when you multiply a number by 10?

	TTh	Th	H	T	U	.	t
a				5	1	.	6
b			4	3	0	.	2
c		8	0	9	0	.	7

2 Multiply each number by 100.
What happens to each digit when you multiply a number by 100?
What did you write in an empty column? Explain why.

	TTh	Th	H	T	U	.	t
a					2	.	5
b				9	0	.	9
c			7	0	0	.	3

3 Find 10 times each mass, and then 100 times each mass.

a 4·7 kg   **b** 30·9 kg   **c** 81·7 kg   **d** 205·3 kg

4 Multiply each number by 1000.
Write each answer in words.

	M	HTh	TTh	Th	H	T	U
a						6	9
b					8	0	2
c				8	0	0	5

Let's play   A game for 2

You need

2 dice

Take turns to:
- Roll both dice.
- Choose 1 number from each box to match the scores on your dice.
- Find the product of the 2 numbers.

The player with the larger product scores 1 point.

The winner is the first to 5 points.

Dice score	Number
⚀	352
⚁	21
⚂	4008
⚃	9
⚄	17 046
⚅	0·7

Dice score	Number
⚀	1000
⚁	10
⚂	100
⚃	100
⚄	1000
⚅	10

Let's practise

1 Divide each number by 10.
What happens to each digit when
you divide a number by 10?

	Th	H	T	U	t	h
a		6	0	0		
b	4	5	0	9		
c		7	8	3	2	

2 Divide each number by 100.
What happens to each digit when
you divide a number by 100?

	Th	H	T	U	t	h
a				3	4	
b		8	7	0		
c	8	0	2	5		

3 Divide each amount of money by 10, 100 and 1000.

a £56 920 **b** £27 810 **c** £892 450 **d** £901 560

4 Divide each number by 1000.
Write each answer in words.

	M	HTh	TTh	Th	H	T	U
a				9	0	0	0
b		5	7	0	0	0	0
c			9	8	0	0	0

Let's play A game for 2

You need
2 dice

Take turns to:
- Roll both dice.
- Choose 1 number from each box
  to match the scores on your dice.
- Divide the number from the first
  box by the number from the
  second.

The player with the smaller answer
scores 1 point.

The winner is the first to 5 points.

Dice score	Number to be divided
⚀	56 000
⚁	690 000
⚂	3000
⚃	24 000
⚄	490 000
⚅	3 209 000

Dice score	Number to divide by
⚀	10
⚁	100
⚂	1000
⚃	10
⚄	100
⚅	1000

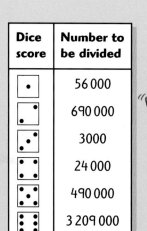

Let's practise

1 Copy each pair of numbers.
Write **<** or **>** to make each statement correct.

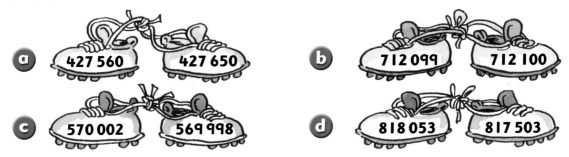

a 427 560 427 650 **b** 712 099 712 100

c 570 002 569 998 **d** 818 053 817 503

2 Write the set of integers that makes each statement correct.

a $15 \leqslant \blacksquare \leqslant 20$ **b** $453 \leqslant \blacksquare \leqslant 460$ **c** $15\,480 \leqslant \blacksquare \leqslant 15\,490$

3 Brian and Sula play a computer game. For each pair of scores write
- who scored more
- a number between the two scores.

a

Brian	Sula
35 781	35 871

c

Brian	Sula
700 456	700 465

b

Brian	Sula
612 809	611 999

d

Brian	Sula
913 000	911 999

Let's investigate

4 **a** Use the digits on the footballs to make 12 different
6-digit numbers between 450 000 and 500 000.

b Write the numbers in order.

Find the pair of numbers with:

c the smallest total **d** the largest total

e the smallest difference **f** the largest difference.

3 4 5 8 9 7

? What if you used the digits on the footballs to make all possible 6-digit
numbers between 450 000 and 460 000? How many would there be?

Let's practise

1 Copy and complete the calculations. Write **>**, **<** or **=** for each ball.

a 400 + 700 ⬯ 2000 − 900   **b** 3 × 450 ⬯ 1150 − 250

c 9500 − 4050 ⬯ 7000 ÷ 2   **d** 5050 ÷ 5 ⬯ 9 × 105

2 **a** There are five multiples of 4 between two numbers that are greater than 50. What could the two numbers be?

b There are three multiples of 7 between two 3-digit numbers that are less than 150. What could the two numbers be?

c There are four multiples of 9 between two 4-digit numbers that are greater than 2000. What could the two numbers be?

3 Copy and complete.

a 48☐1 > 4☐69   **b** 1☐02 < 15☐1   **c** 72 675 < ☐267☐

Let's solve problems

4 Jo says:

> I am thinking of a whole number between 200 000 and 500 000.
> If I double my number the answer is less than 500 000.
> If I halve my number the answer is more than 120 000.
> What could my number be?

Give 10 different possible numbers.

Let's investigate

5 Investigate using these digit cards: 8 5 3 7 4 1

Complete this in as many ways as you can: ☐☐☐ < ☐☐☐

? What if the same cards were used for this? ☐☐☐ > ☐☐☐

Let's practise

1 Copy the calculations and choose the best approximate answer for each.
Write how you rounded the numbers to make your estimate.

a 63 × 42	**240**	**2400**	**24 000**
b 395 × 25	**1000**	**10 000**	**100 000**
c 166 + 293	**350**	**400**	**450**
d 681 − 379	**200**	**300**	**400**
e 578 ÷ 8	**50**	**70**	**90**
f 462 ÷ 5·5	**100**	**150**	**200**

Now use a calculator to find the exact answer to each question.

2 Estimate first and then find the total height of each office block.

a 9 storeys each 2·8 m high

b 7 storeys each 3·2 m high

c 8 storeys each 2·3 m high

d 3 storeys each 3·64 m high

e 5 storeys each 2·57 m high

f 6 storeys each 3·72 m high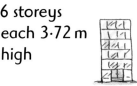

Let's solve problems

3 Estimate answers to these questions. Write how you decided.

a How many 1p coins would make a line 1 km long?

b How many meals will you have eaten before you are 20?

c How many words are there in a story book?

d How many hours of television do you watch in a year?

e How many times will you come to school before you are 16?

f How much water do you drink in a year?

Compare your estimates with those of a friend.

Let's practise

① Write the numbers in order, smallest first.

ⓐ    ⓑ

ⓒ   ⓓ

Let's play   A game for 2

Take turns to choose a number from each bag below.
- Find the difference between them.
- If the answer is in the grid, cover it with a counter.

The winner is the first with 4 counters in a vertical, horizontal or diagonal line.

You need

counters in 2 colours

1	7	2	24	8	3
7	37	9	10	23	33
3	28	11	20	25	15
16	21	27	2	18	13
12	3	17	12	7	11
25	20	4	1	14	6

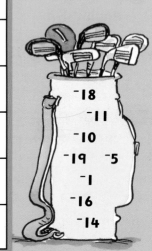

Let's investigate

② Look at this equation: + = 12

 and stand for positive or negative whole numbers.

Investigate possible values for and .
What do you notice?

⍰ What if the equation was −  = 12 ?

Let's practise

1 Copy, complete and continue for 4 more rows.

a
$1 \times 1 =$
$2 \times 2 =$
$3 \times 3 =$
$4 \times 4 =$
$5 \times 5 =$
$6 \times 6 =$

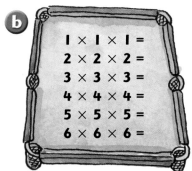

b
$1 \times 1 \times 1 =$
$2 \times 2 \times 2 =$
$3 \times 3 \times 3 =$
$4 \times 4 \times 4 =$
$5 \times 5 \times 5 =$
$6 \times 6 \times 6 =$

c
$1 \times 1 \times 1 \times 1 =$
$2 \times 2 \times 2 \times 2 =$
$3 \times 3 \times 3 \times 3 =$
$4 \times 4 \times 4 \times 4 =$
$5 \times 5 \times 5 \times 5 =$
$6 \times 6 \times 6 \times 6 =$

Write about any patterns you notice.

2 Copy, complete and continue.

a
$2^2 - 1^2 =$
$3^2 - 2^2 =$
$4^2 - 3^2 =$
$5^2 - 4^2 =$

b
$(2 \times 2 \times 2) - (1 \times 1 \times 1) =$
$(3 \times 3 \times 3) - (2 \times 2 \times 2) =$
$(4 \times 4 \times 4) - (3 \times 3 \times 3) =$
$(5 \times 5 \times 5) - (4 \times 4 \times 4) =$

c
$(2 \times 2 \times 2 \times 2) - (1 \times 1 \times 1 \times 1) =$
$(3 \times 3 \times 3 \times 3) - (2 \times 2 \times 2 \times 2) =$
$(4 \times 4 \times 4 \times 4) - (3 \times 3 \times 3 \times 3) =$
$(5 \times 5 \times 5 \times 5) - (4 \times 4 \times 4 \times 4) =$

Write about any patterns you notice.

Let's investigate

3 Gary uses coloured pegs to make a sequence of 'empty' squares.

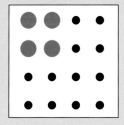 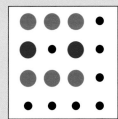 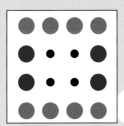 

a What is the number sequence made by the red pegs?

b What is the number sequence made by the blue pegs?

c What is the sequence made by the total number of pegs?

d How are these 3 sequences related?

? What if Gary's 'empty' squares were 'empty' triangles?

Let's practise

1 Copy and continue each sequence
until you reach a number greater than 100.

a 7   13   19   25   ⬛ ⬛ ⬛ ...

b 5   14   23   32   ⬛ ⬛ ⬛ ...

c 6   14   22   30   ⬛ ⬛ ⬛ ...

Let's investigate

2 Work with a partner.

- Use counters to build a sequence of triangles.
  Make each row a different colour.

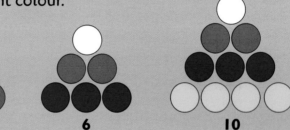

  1   3   6   10

- Continue the sequence for 4 more triangular numbers.

- Write the sequence of triangular numbers until you
  reach a number greater than 100.

- Here is the start of the sequence of square numbers:

  1   4   9   16   25 ...

  How many square numbers between 1 and 200 are also triangular numbers?

3 Harry had 3 different colours of counters.
He made 3 different pairs using the 3 colours.

- Investigate making different pairs using 4, 5, 6, 7, ... colours.

- Copy this table and record your results.

Number of colours	2	3	4	5	6	7
Number of pairs		3				

- Write about any patterns you notice.

Let's practise

1 Start from 0 and write a sequence of
8 numbers counting on in steps of

   a 0·2   **b** 0·5

2 Start from 10 and write a sequence of
8 numbers counting back in steps of

   a 0·1   **b** 0·25

3 Start from 0. Write 2 sequences of your own.

Let's play   A game for 2

- Use your paper circle to make a spinner like this one.
- Each start from 5.
- Take turns to spin the clip on the spinner.
- Follow the instructions on the spinner.
- Each time, continue counting from the last number on your previous turn.
- The winner is the first to reach 8.
- Play again.
- Invent a way to record the game.

You need

a paper circle divided
into 6 equal sections,
a paper clip, a pencil

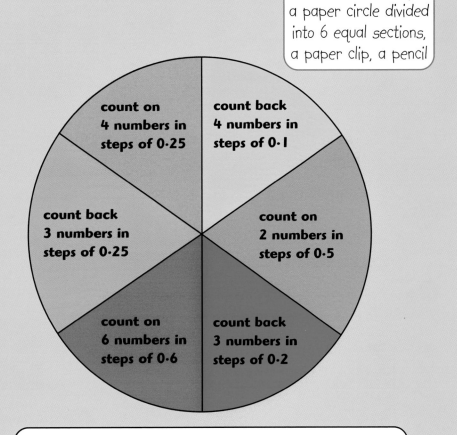

To spin the clip:
- Put the paper clip in the middle of the spinner.
- Put the point of a pencil through the paper clip in the middle of the spinner.
- Flick the clip around the spinner.

Let's practise

1 Write all the numbers in this square that are multiples of

a 3 and 5 **b** 2 and 7

c 9 and 4.

2 Now write 2 numbers between 300 and 400 that are multiples of

a 3 and 5 **b** 2 and 7

c 9 and 4.

3 Write whether each statement about the square is true or false.

a There are more odd numbers than even numbers.

b All the multiples of 6 are also multiples of 3.

c The square numbers make a line.

×	1	2	3	4	5	6	7	8	9	10
1	1	2	3	4	5	6	7	8	9	10
2	2	4	6	8	10	12	14	16	18	20
3	3	6	9	12	15	18	21	24	27	30
4	4	8	12	16	20	24	28	32	36	40
5	5	10	15	20	25	30	35	40	45	50
6	6	12	18	24	30	36	42	48	54	60
7	7	14	21	28	35	42	49	56	63	70
8	8	16	24	32	40	48	56	64	72	80
9	9	18	27	36	45	54	63	72	81	90
10	10	20	30	40	50	60	70	80	90	100

Let's investigate

4 ● Copy any 2 x 2 square of numbers from the multiplication square above.

● Add each diagonal:

● Investigate other 2 x 2 squares of numbers.

● Write about what you notice. Explain why this happens.

? What if you find the sum of the 3 numbers in each diagonal of a 3 x 3 square? ... a 4 x 4 square?

Let's practise

Checklist A

If a number is even, it is a multiple of 2.

If its last 2 digits are a multiple of 4, then the number is a multiple of 4.

If its last 3 digits are a multiple of 8, then the number is a multiple of 8.

Checklist B

Add the digits.

If the answer is a multiple of 3, then the number is a multiple of 3.

If the answer is a multiple of 3 and the original number is even, then that number is a multiple of 6.

If the answer is a multiple of 9, then the number is a multiple of 9.

1 Use the checklists above to test 124 for divisibility.
- Which numbers from 2 to 10 is 124 divisible by?
- Which numbers from 2 to 10 is 124 not divisible by?

2 Do this again for:

   a 936   **b** 531   **c** 284   **d** 115   **e** 1350.

Let's investigate

3
- Investigate numbers between 1000 and 1200 that are divisible by 6, by 8 and by both 6 and 8.
- Show your results on a Venn diagram.

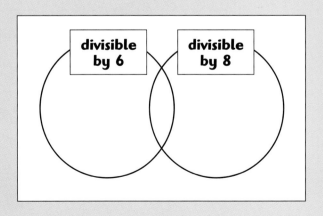

? What if the numbers are between 2000 and 2200?

Let's practise

1 Bimla lists the first ten multiples of 2 and of 3.

| multiples of 2: | 2 | 4 | 6 | 8 | 10 | 12 | 14 | 16 | 18 | 20 |
| multiples of 3: | 3 | 6 | 9 | 12 | 15 | 18 | 21 | 24 | 27 | 30 |

a Which numbers listed are multiples of both 2 and 3?

b Write the next five common multiples of 2 and 3.

c What is the lowest common multiple of 2 and 3?

2 Find the first ten common multiples of:

a 3 and 4   **b** 6 and 8   **c** 3 and 5   **d** 2 and 7.

3 What is the lowest common multiple of:

a 2 and 5   **b** 3 and 7   **c** 4 and 8   **d** 6 and 9?

Let's solve problems

4 **a** Find the number.

I am a multiple of 2 and 5. My digits add up to 2. Who am I?

Some riddles have more than one answer!

b Invent 3 number riddles of your own.
Try them out on some friends.

Let's practise

1 What is the square of each number?

a 7, 70, 700, 7000

b 11, 110, 1100, 11 000

Let's play A game for 2

You need

2 dice

- Player 1 rolls the dice.
- Use the score to make two 2-digit numbers.
- Choose which 2-digit number to use.
- Estimate the square of your number.
- Player 2 uses the calculator to find the exact square.
- You score the difference between your estimate and the exact square.
- Swap roles.

The winner is the player with the smaller difference.

For example:

can be 25 or 52.

Let's investigate

2 Joshua discovers that 12 can be written as the difference between two square numbers:

$$12 = 4^2 - 2^2$$

Investigate writing the numbers from 1 to 50 as the difference between two square numbers.

? What if you tried to write the numbers from 1 to 50 as the sum of two square numbers?

Let's practise

1 Look at these 5 numbers:

Write all the numbers that are:

a divisible by 8

b divisible by 4

c divisible by 2

d divisible by 3

e divisible by 3 and 2

f divisible by 3 and 4

g divisible by 3 and 5

h divisible only by 1 and itself.

2 **a** Find all the prime numbers between
1 and 10, 10 and 20, 20 and 30, and so on,
up to 90 and 100.

b How many numbers in each decade are prime?
Write about any patterns you notice.

> Remember:
> A prime number has
> only two factors: the
> number and itself.
>
> 1 to 10 is one decade, 11 to
> 20 is another decade, ...

Let's investigate

3 ● Copy this grid onto squared paper.

● Colour each square that contains
a prime number.

● Write about what you notice.

● Investigate what happens if you extend
the grid to 100.

You need

2 cm squared paper

1	2	3	4	5	6
7	8	9	10	11	12
13	14	15	16	17	18
19	20	21	22	23	24
25	26	27	28	29	30

? What if the number grid has 7, 8 or 9 squares
in each row?

Let's practise

1 This is Euan's method for finding the prime factors of 40.

Step 1
Find a factor pair of 40, for example, 4 and 10.

Step 2
Look for factor pairs of 4 and 10.

Step 3
Continue until your answers are all prime numbers.

$2 \times 2 \times 2 \times 5 = 40$

These are the prime factors of 40.

a Find the prime factors of each of these numbers.

b Which of the numbers has the most prime factors?

c Which has the fewest?

2 Find numbers that have only 2 prime factors.

Let's investigate

3 Investigate numbers less than 100 that have 3, 4, 5 or 6 prime factors.

Let's practise

1 Copy and complete.

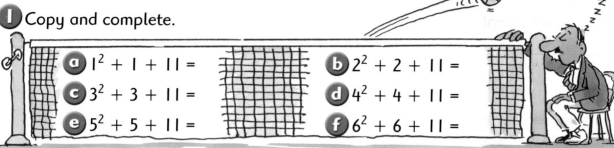

(a) $1^2 + 1 + 11 =$ (b) $2^2 + 2 + 11 =$

(c) $3^2 + 3 + 11 =$ (d) $4^2 + 4 + 11 =$

(e) $5^2 + 5 + 11 =$ (f) $6^2 + 6 + 11 =$

All the answers are odd numbers. They also have another name. What is it?

2 Copy and complete.

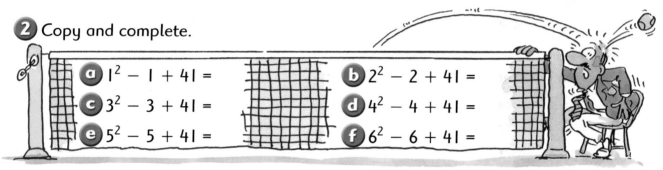

(a) $1^2 - 1 + 41 =$ (b) $2^2 - 2 + 41 =$

(c) $3^2 - 3 + 41 =$ (d) $4^2 - 4 + 41 =$

(e) $5^2 - 5 + 41 =$ (f) $6^2 - 6 + 41 =$

Again the answers are odd numbers. What else are they?

Let's investigate

3 Julie found the factors of 21 and 12.

21 has four factors:
1, 3, 7, 21

12 has six factors:
1, 2, 3, 4, 6, 12

Investigate which 2-digit number has the most factors.

? What if you investigated which 2-digit numbers have fewest factors?

Let's practise

1 Copy and complete.

a $\frac{23}{6} = \boxed{}\frac{5}{6}$ **b** $\frac{\boxed{}}{3} = 15\frac{2}{3}$ **c** $\frac{33}{\boxed{}} = 8\frac{\boxed{}}{4}$ **d** $5\frac{\boxed{}}{\boxed{}} = \frac{29}{5}$ **e** $\boxed{}\frac{3}{\boxed{}} = \frac{63}{10}$

Let's play A game for 1

Roll all 3 dice.

- Use the two 1–6 dice to make two 2-digit numbers. These are your numerators.
- The number on the 7–12 dice is your denominator.
- Use the numerators and denominator to make 2 improper fractions.
- Change each fraction to a mixed number.
- If one of the mixed numbers is on the grid, cover it with a counter.
- Can you cover 4 mixed numbers in a line in any direction?

$3\frac{8}{9}$	$7\frac{5}{7}$	$6\frac{3}{8}$	$2\frac{4}{9}$
$2\frac{5}{8}$	$1\frac{3}{10}$	$3\frac{10}{11}$	$1\frac{3}{12}$
$6\frac{7}{9}$	$3\frac{5}{7}$	$1\frac{6}{10}$	$4\frac{3}{8}$
$1\frac{4}{7}$	$2\frac{3}{9}$	$3\frac{3}{8}$	$7\frac{4}{7}$

You need

two 1–6 dice, one 7–12 dice, counters

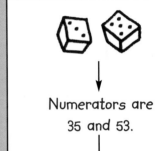

Numerators are 35 and 53.

9

Denominator is 9.

The two improper fractions are $\frac{35}{9}$ and $\frac{53}{9}$.

Let's investigate

2 Use only prime numbers from 3 to 19.
The numerator is the sum of 2 of the prime numbers, and the denominator is a different prime number.

Investigate making whole numbers this way.

? What if the numerator is the sum of 3 prime numbers and the denominator is a different prime number?

Let's practise

1 Copy and complete.

a half of $\frac{1}{4}$ is ▨   **b** half of $\frac{1}{6}$ is ▨   **c** half of $\frac{1}{8}$ is ▨

d ▨ is a half of $\frac{1}{4}$ **e** ▨ is a half of $\frac{1}{5}$ **f** ▨ is a half of $\frac{1}{3}$

2 Ivan uses the fraction wall to write these statements about $\frac{1}{4}$ and $\frac{1}{8}$:

$\frac{1}{4}$ is twice $\frac{1}{8}$ $\frac{1}{8}$ is half of $\frac{1}{4}$

1 whole									
$\frac{1}{2}$									
$\frac{1}{4}$									
$\frac{1}{8}$									
$\frac{1}{3}$									
$\frac{1}{6}$									
$\frac{1}{5}$									
$\frac{1}{10}$									

Write 2 statements for each pair of fractions.

a $\frac{1}{5}$ and $\frac{1}{10}$ **b** $\frac{1}{2}$ and $\frac{1}{8}$ **c** $\frac{1}{2}$ and $\frac{1}{6}$ **d** $\frac{3}{4}$ and $\frac{3}{8}$ **e** $\frac{2}{3}$ and $\frac{1}{6}$

Let's solve problems

3 **a** At the netball match, Jackie had halves of oranges.
Each orange half was shared equally between 3 players.
What fraction of a whole orange did each player eat?

b Ben was asked to mark out badminton courts in one half of the
sports hall. Each court covered $\frac{1}{8}$ of the whole hall.
How many courts could he mark out?

c Mo used three quarters of the athletics track to set up 2 identical
obstacle courses.
What fraction of the whole track did one obstacle course use?

Let's practise

1 Copy and complete.

a $\frac{2}{4} = \frac{\square}{2}$ **b** $\frac{4}{10} = \frac{\square}{5}$ **c** $\frac{2}{6} = \frac{\square}{3}$

d $\frac{2}{8} = \frac{1}{\square}$ **e** $\frac{\square}{10} = \frac{2}{\square}$ **f** $\frac{4}{\square} = \frac{\square}{2}$

2 Cancel each fraction.

a $\frac{3}{6}$ **b** $\frac{6}{8}$ **c** $\frac{24}{30}$ **d** $\frac{7}{14}$

e $\frac{5}{15}$ **f** $\frac{10}{16}$ **g** $\frac{16}{20}$ **h** $\frac{25}{100}$

Let's investigate

3 Sam chose 4 numbers from these to make this equivalent fraction statement:

$$\frac{1}{2} = \frac{3}{6}$$

Investigate making as many equivalent fraction statements as you can by choosing 4 different numbers each time.

? What if you used six different numbers each time from 1 to 20 to make equivalent fraction statements with three fractions?

$$\frac{1}{4} = \frac{2}{8} = \frac{3}{12}$$

Let's practise

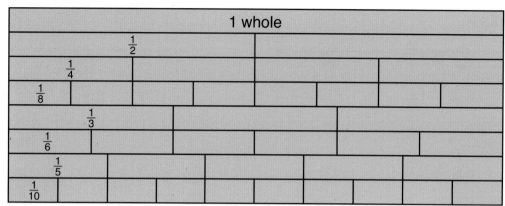

| 1 whole |
| $\frac{1}{2}$ |
| $\frac{1}{4}$ |
| $\frac{1}{8}$ |
| $\frac{1}{3}$ |
| $\frac{1}{6}$ |
| $\frac{1}{5}$ |
| $\frac{1}{10}$ |

The fraction wall will help you.

1 Write these fractions in order, smallest first.

$$\frac{1}{2} \qquad \frac{3}{8} \qquad \frac{2}{3} \qquad \frac{5}{6} \qquad \frac{3}{10} \qquad \frac{1}{4} \qquad \frac{2}{5}$$

2 Write the fractions in each pair as fractions with the same denominator. Circle the larger fraction in each pair.

a $\frac{1}{2}$ and $\frac{3}{4}$ **b** $\frac{3}{5}$ and $\frac{1}{2}$ **c** $\frac{1}{4}$ and $\frac{1}{5}$

d $\frac{2}{3}$ and $\frac{3}{4}$ **e** $\frac{2}{5}$ and $\frac{2}{3}$ **f** $\frac{3}{8}$ and $\frac{3}{4}$

Let's investigate

$\frac{1}{6}$ $\frac{2}{6}$ $\frac{3}{6}$ $\frac{4}{6}$ $\frac{5}{6}$

3 a List the fractions less than 1 that have a denominator of 6. Reduce each one to its simplest equivalent fraction.

b How many reduce to a denominator that is not 6?

c How many still have a denominator of 6?

4 a Investigate the sets of fractions with denominators 4, 5, 7, 8, 9, 10, ...

b What is special about the denominators in the sets that have no fractions that can be reduced?

Let's practise

1 Copy and complete.

a $\frac{1}{5}$ of 45 = 45 ÷ ☐ = ☐

b 63 ÷ 8 = $\frac{63}{☐}$ = 7$\frac{☐}{☐}$

c 71 ÷ ☐ = $\frac{71}{10}$ = ☐$\frac{1}{10}$

d $\frac{1}{100}$ of 500 = ☐ ÷ ☐ = ☐

e ☐ ÷ ☐ = $\frac{62}{5}$ = ☐$\frac{☐}{☐}$

f 19 ÷ ☐ = $\frac{☐}{☐}$ = 2$\frac{3}{8}$

2 Copy and complete.

a $\frac{3}{4}$ of 24 = ☐

b $\frac{5}{8}$ of 56 = ☐

c $\frac{5}{7}$ of 63 = ☐

d $\frac{5}{6}$ of 72 = ☐

e $\frac{2}{3}$ of 90 litres = ☐

f $\frac{3}{100}$ of 800 metres = ☐

g $\frac{7}{8}$ of 96 grams = ☐

h $\frac{9}{100}$ of 1000 kg = ☐

i $\frac{3}{10}$ of 1 hour = ☐

Let's solve problems

3 At the races, 3 litres of orange juice
are shared equally between 10 jockeys.

a What fraction of a litre does each jockey get?

b How much juice is that in millilitres?

4 **a** Jim's horse was in the lead for the first 50 m of the race.
What fraction of a kilometre is 50 m?

b Two thirds of the 42 starters finished the race.
How many did not finish?

5 Star Blazer had trained hard from the start of April to the
end of June.

a For how many months was Star Blazer in training?

b What fraction of a year is that?

c For how many days was Star Blazer in training?

d What fraction of a year is that?

Let's practise

1 A ▮▮□▮▮□▮▮▮□▮□ B ▮□□▮▮□▮□▮▮□▮□

C ▮▮▮□▮▮▮□▮▮▮□▮▮▮□

Copy and complete each statement.

Pattern A: There are ▮ blue tiles for every ▮ white tile.

Pattern B: There are ▮ white tiles in every ▮ tiles.

Pattern C: There are ▮ blue tiles in every ▮ tiles.

2 A pattern has blue and red tiles.
The proportion of blue tiles is 1 in every 4 tiles.
Draw the pattern, showing 12 tiles altogether.

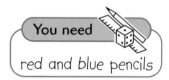

You need

red and blue pencils

3 Draw a pattern to match each statement and answer the questions.

a A pattern of blue and red tiles has 1 blue tile for every 2 red tiles.
What is the proportion of red tiles in the pattern?
What fraction of the pattern is red?

b A pattern of red and blue tiles has 1 red tile for every 3 blue tiles.
What is the proportion of blue tiles in the pattern?
What fraction of the pattern is blue?

Let's solve problems

4 At the athletics club there are 3 boys for every 2 girls.
There are 40 children at the club. How many boys are there?

5 In the field sports section there is 1 javelin thrower for every 3 shot putters.
There are 16 children in the field sports section.

a What is the proportion of shot putters?
Give your answer
as a fraction.

b How many
javelin throwers
are there?

Let's practise

1 Copy each number. Write the value of the red digits in words.

a 1·463   **b** 4·217   **c** 2·956   **d** 3·485

e 5·392   **f** 6·509   **g** 9·214   **h** 7·812

2 Copy and write each number in figures as a decimal.

a four tenths and six thousandths

b seventeen thousandths

c one tenth five hundredths and nine thousandths

d eight tenths and three thousandths

e fourteen and thirty-seven thousandths

3 Copy and write each number in words.

a 0·036   **b** 3·844   **c** 0·903   **d** 1·005   **e** 17·102

Let's play   A game for 1

- Roll the 4 dice and record each digit.
- Arrange the digits to make a number with 3 decimal places.
- Change your number to 1, using these rules and the fewest possible operations.

You need

four 1–6 dice

Rules

- You may add or subtract 0·1, 0·01, 0·001, 0·5, 0·05, or 0·005 only.
- You may multiply or divide by 10 or 100.
- You must only do one operation at a time and then record the result.
- You must not let your number become negative.

1·441
1·441 − 0·5 = 0·941
0·941 + 0·1 = 1·041
1·041 ...

How many operations did you use?

Let's practise

1 Copy each sequence, then write 4 more numbers.

a 1·80, 1·82, 1·84, ...　　**b** 3·93, 3·95, 3·97, ...　　**c** 7·06, 7·04, 7·02, ...

d 2·67, 2·65, 2·63, ...　　**e** 6·92, 6·94, 6·96, ...　　**f** 5·77, 5·75, 5·73, ...

2 Write each set of numbers in order, from largest to smallest.

a 5·43, 5·34, 5·62, 15·05, 5·09　　　　**b** 1·5, 1·25, 1·425, 1·3, 1·285

3 Write each set of numbers in order, from smallest to largest.

a 4·325, 4·523, 4·253, 4·352, 4·532　　　　**b** 8·836, 8·386, 8·863, 8·638, 8·368

Let's solve problems

4 In the 'Across Australia' rally, the distances below were recorded.
Suggest an exact distance each team could have driven.

a red team: between 324·35 miles and 324·36 miles

b blue team: between 497·43 miles and 497·44 miles

c purple team: between 465·25 miles and 465·26 miles

d yellow team: between 393·99 miles and 394·00 miles

5 In a triathlon race, competitors had to swim 2·112 km,
cycle 2·962 km and run 2·438 km. The winner took 45·12 minutes.
The fifth place time was 47·38 minutes.

a Write the 3 distances in order, from the longest to shortest.

b Suggest times for the second, third and fourth places.

6 During a weightlifting competition, these lifts were recorded.

50·575 kg　　55·645 kg　　45·385 kg　　54·885 kg　　55·685 kg

Which weights won the gold, silver and bronze medals?

Let's practise

1 Each number has been rounded to the nearest tenth.
Copy and complete by writing a digit that
could be under each hoof print.

a 3·6 ⊃ → 3·7 **b** 9· ⊃ 2 → 9·4 **c** 4·6 ⊃ → 4·6²

d 2·3 ⊃ → 2·4 **e** 5· ⊃⊃ → 5·7 **f** ⊃·⊃ 7 → 8·2

g 7· ⊃⊃ → 7·8 **h** 6·2 ⊃ → 6·3 **i** ⊃·⊃⊃ → 1·9

2 Round each of the following to the nearest tenth.

a 35·38 kg **b** 12·46 min **c** 81·82 ml **d** 10·49 sec

e 142·64 cm **f** 109·27 m **g** 151·78 km **h** £135·91

3 Write all the numbers with 2 decimal places that would give each of the following
answers when rounded to the nearest tenth.

a 1·6 **b** 7·8 **c** 4·2 **d** 5·0

4 Write ten numbers with 2 decimal places that would give each of the following
answers when rounded to the nearest whole number.

a 6 **b** 11 **c** 1 **d** 80

Let's investigate 🖩

5 ● Divide a 1-digit number by another 1-digit number.

● Only record those that give an answer with exactly
2 decimal places.

● Round your answers to 1 decimal place.

● Write about any patterns you can see. Make predictions.

? What if you divide a 2-digit number by a 1-digit number
and use the same rules?

Let's practise

1 Copy and complete.

a $0.5 = \frac{\square}{2}$ **b** $0.7\square = \frac{3}{4}$ **c** $0.\square 3 = \frac{3}{\square}$ **d** $\frac{\square}{5} = 0.\square$

2 Copy each decimal number. Write it as a mixed number in its simplest form.

a 4·35   **b** 1·2   **c** 6·05   **d** 8·125   **e** 2·25

Let's solve problems

3 Here are team results from an athletics meeting.

a Write them as mixed numbers in their simplest form.

b Place them in order of gold, silver and bronze for each event.

Discus		High jump		Long jump	

Discus		**High jump**		**Long jump**	
red	22·005 m	red	1·535 m	red	3·575 m
blue	24·105 m	blue	1·605 m	blue	3·455 m
green	22·115 m	green	1·065 m	green	3·475 m
yellow	23·975 m	yellow	1·955 m	yellow	3·755 m

4 Here are the team results from the track events, measured in seconds (s).

a Write them as decimal numbers.

b Place them in order of gold, silver and bronze for each event.

100 m

400 m hurdles

100 m		**400 m hurdles**	
red	$10\frac{32}{1000}$ s	red	$45\frac{261}{1000}$ s
blue	$11\frac{257}{1000}$ s	blue	$45\frac{749}{1000}$ s
green	$10\frac{305}{1000}$ s	green	$45\frac{3}{1000}$ s
yellow	$11\frac{145}{1000}$ s	yellow	$45\frac{48}{1000}$ s

Let's practise

1 Copy each fraction and write it as a decimal and a percentage.

a $\frac{30}{100}$ **b** $\frac{45}{100}$ **c** $\frac{7}{10}$ **d** $\frac{1}{2}$

e $\frac{3}{4}$ **f** $\frac{1}{5}$ **g** $\frac{7}{25}$ **h** $\frac{19}{20}$

2 Use your answers to question 1. Write:

a the fraction closest to $\frac{1}{3}$

b all the fractions between 25% and 50%

c all the percentages less than $\frac{2}{3}$

d all the percentages between $\frac{2}{3}$ and $\frac{3}{4}$

e all the fractions less than 33%

f all the percentages between $\frac{1}{10}$ and $\frac{2}{5}$.

Let's solve problems

3 At a swimming gala the judges awarded the cup for each race to the school with the best percentage success rate.

a In the 500 m freestyle, children had to finish.

8 out of 20 swimmers finished for school A, and 10 out of 30 for school B.

Which school won the cup?

Explain how you decided.

b The 60 m butterfly race had to be completed in less than 2 minutes.

12 out of 16 swimmers for school C beat the time limit.

24 out of 30 for school D beat the time limit.

18 out of 20 for school E beat the time limit.

Which school won the cup?

Explain how you decided.

c In the relay race, every length had to be swum in less than 1 minute.

8 out of 27 swimmers were successful for school A.

12 out of 20 were successful for school C.

6 out of 11 were successful for school D.

Which school won the cup?

Explain how you decided.

Let's practise

1 **a** Which of these percentages is equivalent to 0·59?

    5·9%   59%   0·59%   590%

b Which of these decimals is equivalent to 34%?

    3·4   34·0   0·34   0·034

c Which of these percentages is approximately $\frac{2}{3}$?

    33%   67%   55%   60%

d Write each number that is greater than $\frac{1}{2}$.

    0·75 $\frac{5}{8}$ 45% $\frac{5}{10}$ 51%   0·4 $\frac{2}{5}$ 80%

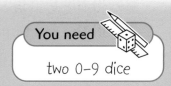

Let's play   A game for 1

> **You need**
>
> two 0–9 dice

- Start with 10 points.
- Roll both dice. If you get a zero, roll that dice again.
- Use the numbers to make a fraction, with the smaller number as the numerator.
- Make 6 fractions in this way.
- Rewrite the fractions in order, smallest to largest. Do not use the calculator. Estimate if you need to.
- Now use the calculator to convert your fractions to decimal fractions. Record the first 2 decimal places only.
- Convert your decimal fractions to percentages. Keep a clear record of your work.

$\frac{1}{7}$	$\frac{2}{9}$	$\frac{3}{8}$	$\frac{3}{7}$	$\frac{1}{3}$	$\frac{8}{9}$
0·14	0·22	0·38	0·43	0·33	0·89
14%	22%	38%	43%	33%	89%

- Lose 1 point for every fraction that is in the wrong place. If all the fractions are in the correct order, keep all your points.
- Play 4 more times.

   How many points are left at the end of all 5 rounds?

   Did your estimation improve as you played?

Let's practise

1 Write the simplest equivalent fraction for each percentage.

a 25% **b** 30% **c** 75% **d** 40%

e 10% **f** 60% **g** 80% **h** 20%

2 Copy and find the percentages.

a 30% of 5 kg **b** 20% of 30 cm **c** 60% of £50 **d** 10% of 65 m

e 25% of £420 **f** 70% of 500 g **g** 40% of 3 litres **h** 75% of 168 g

Let's solve problems

3 **a** A racing bike costs £450.
It has a 20% discount in a sale.
What is its price?

b A surfing wetsuit costs £360.
It has a 25% discount in a sale.
What is its price?

c The sports shop is having a clearance sale.
If you buy 3 items that total £640,
you can have a discount of 40%.
How much would you pay for the 3 items?

d Write some discount problems for a friend to
solve. Make sure you know the answers.

Let's investigate

4 Here is an incomplete percentage statement: ▢ % of £ ▲ = £ ⬭

Investigate which numbers to choose from
these matching shapes to make 10 different correct statements.

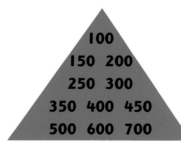

10	20	25
30	40	50
60	70	75
80	90

100
150 200
250 300
350 400 450
500 600 700

50 60 90 100
135 140 150
225 420

Let's practise

1 Copy and find the percentages.

a 10% of 200 kg   **b** 50% of £340   **c** 25% of 28 m   **d** 50% of 104 g

e 25% of 52p   **f** 10% of 890 ml   **g** 20% of £500   **h** 75% of 12 cm

Let's play   **A game for 2**

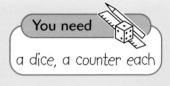

You need

a dice, a counter each

- You each start with £1000.
  Keep a record of your money as you play.

- Start at 1 on the board and roll the dice.
  Move your counter a matching number of places.

- If you land on a cable car, find 40% of your money.
  Add it on as profit. Round your total to the
  nearest £10.

40% of £1000 is £400
£1000 + £400 = £1400

20% of £1400 is £280
£1400 − £280 = £1120

- If you land on a ski slope, find 20% of your money.
  Subtract this as a loss. Round your total to the
  nearest £10.

When you have both reached 60, the player with more
money wins.

More than £1000 is a profit. Less than £1000 is a loss.

60	59	58	57	56	55	54	53	52	51
41	42	43	44	45	46	47	48	49	50
40	39	38	37	36	35	34	33	32	31
21	22	23	24	25	26	27	28	29	30
20	19	18	17	16	15	14	13	12	11
1	2	3	4	5	6	7	8	9	10

Let's practise

1 **a** Subtract 2250 from 8500.
b Add 4256 to 3530.

c ▢ + 1475 = 5829
d ▢ − 1525 = 5367

e Decrease 4027 by 360.
f Increase 2946 by 398.

2 Write what has been added to or subtracted from each number to make the next.

a 7000 → 3785 → 4053 → 9999 → 3987

b 3750 → 7953 → 9015 → 2946 → 6026

Let's solve problems

3 These football teams have travelled abroad to play matches.
The distance travelled on the last 3 trips is shown beneath each team.

a Find the total distance for each team.

1042 km   2748 km   1116 km

2126 km   2256 km   1148 km

809 km   3628 km   3997 km

2657 km   1524 km   2815 km

Which team has travelled:

b the furthest

c about 7000 km

d 624 km more than Town

e 2090 km less than County?

Let's practise

1 Use mental methods to add each of these to 571.
Record each addition.

a 29   **b** 71   **c** 197   **d** 405   **e** 691

f 1997   **g** 3005   **h** 2989   **i** 7001   **j** 6985

k 3·9   **l** 6·1   **m** 8·9   **n** 15·9   **o** 17·1

2 • Choose any start number. Follow this trail.

Think of any number — Add 2999 to it — Subtract 39 — Add 4·1 — Subtract 7·9 — Subtract 899 — Add 0·8 — Subtract 58 — Subtract the number you first thought of

- Record each calculation.
  What number do you end up with?
- Try this for other start numbers, including decimals.

3 Write 5 pairs of numbers with a difference of 2985.
None of your numbers should be less than 1500.

Let's investigate

4 △ and ☐ stand for numbers.

The number △ is between 46 and 58, and △ − ☐ = 7·9

Investigate what △ and ☐ could be. List your findings in a table.

△	☐
47	39·1

? What if △ − ☐ = 8·9?

Let's practise

1 Each symbol stands for one of the numbers 1 to 10. They are not in order.

2		4						10	

Copy the table. Use these equations to find what each symbol stands for.

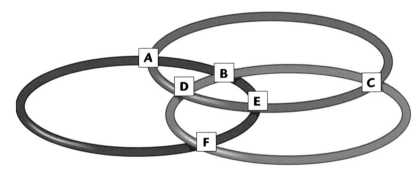

2 The letters A to F stand for different multiples of 10.
The numbers on each hoop have a total of 300.

A D B E C F

a Find one solution for what numbers A to F could be.

b Find as many different solutions as you can.

3 Use the numbers in the bag.

18 20 29 4 3 13 14 8 12 16

a Find two numbers with a sum of 45.

b Find three sets of three numbers, each with a sum of 45.

c Find four sets of four numbers, each with a sum of 45.

Let's investigate

4 The number 45 is the sum of two consecutive numbers (22, 23).
It is also the sum of three consecutive numbers (14, 15, 16).
The number 54 is the sum of four consecutive numbers (12, 13, 14, 15).
Investigate writing every whole number between 45 and 55 as the sum
of two, three or four consecutive numbers.

Let's practise

1 a Find 2 numbers, one on the inner wheel and one on the outer wheel, with a difference that is between 3000 and 5000.

b Find as many pairs as you can.

2 Each javelin throw is measured in metres. How far short of the next whole number of metres is each throw?

Throw of 7·85 m → 7·85 m + 0·15 m = 8 m

a 16·8 m   **b** 22·64 m   **c** 28·78 m   **d** 37·07 m   **e** 46·36 m

3 a Arrange the digits 6 7 8 to complete these decimal numbers:

0 · □ and 0 · □ □

Find their total and their difference.

b Find 5 more ways of doing this.

Let's investigate

4 Here is a list of the prime numbers between 1 and 50:

2, 3, 5, 7, 11, 13, 17, 19, 23, 29, 31, 37, 41, 43, 47

- The sum of the two prime numbers 7 and 13 is 20. Investigate writing even numbers between 20 and 50 as the sum of two prime numbers.

- Which even numbers can be written in more than one way as the sum of two prime numbers?

? What if you investigated numbers greater than 50?

Wheel numbers: 6700, 5700, 9800, 2300, 8800, 3300, 8500, 6600, 4900, 7500, 5600, 5900

Let's practise

1 Estimate which sum is greatest.
Copy each question and calculate the answer.

a
```
  8 5 8 7
+ 2 2 7 5
```

b
```
  7 6 2 8
+ 4 5 9 4
```

c
```
  3 7 3 6
+ 6 6 6 5
```

d
```
  6 3 5 9
+ 5 8 5 9
```

Check your answers using subtraction.

Let's play A game for 2

- Shuffle the cards and place them face down.
- Each player takes four cards and makes
  a 4-digit number with them.
- Add 4687 to your number.
- Each player scores:
  1 point if there is a 3 in their answer.
  2 points if there are two 3s in their answer.
  3 points if there are three 3s in their answer.

The first to reach 5 points is the winner.

You need

two sets of 0–9
digit cards

| 5 | 2 | 6 | 4 |

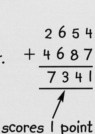

```
  2 6 5 4      or
+ 4 6 8 7
  7 3 4 1
```

scores 1 point

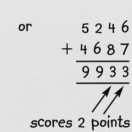

```
  5 2 4 6
+ 4 6 8 7
  9 9 3 3
```

scores 2 points

Let's investigate

2 Lauren is investigating with 4-digit numbers.

First I reversed the digits of my number
to make a new number. Then I found the
total of the two numbers. I discovered
that the total is divisible by 11.

Try this with other 4-digit numbers.
What do you notice?

? What if you used 2-, 3- or 5-digit numbers?

```
  1 6 8 5
+ 5 8 6 1
  7 5 4 6
```

```
       6 8 6
 1 1 ) 7 5 4 6
       6 6
       9 4
       8 8
          6 6
          6 6
          0
```

Let's practise

1 Use a written method to find the total of the 4 numbers in each group of cars.

a

1255 846
5437 4783

b
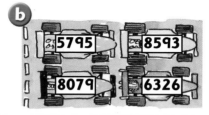
5795 8593
8079 6326

c
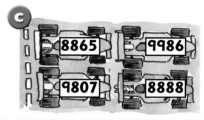
8865 9986
9807 8888

Let's solve problems

2 These racing cars are travelling at very high speeds.
The number of metres they travel each minute is recorded.

	Car 1	Car 2	Car 3	Car 4
1st minute	3640 m	4850 m	3728 m	4255 m
2nd minute	3836 m	4568 m	3768 m	2535 m
3rd minute	2945 m	3058 m	4797 m	3957 m
4th minute	4013 m	2567 m	4879 m	4264 m
5th minute	4274 m	2748 m	4678 m	4634 m

a Which car has travelled the furthest after 5 minutes?

b Write the order of the 4 cars at the end of 5 minutes.

3 This table shows the prize money awarded to 4 tennis players at 5 different tournaments.

Tom	£387	£1378	£4587	£28	£628
Anna	£5785	£536	£58	£218	£5637
Ted	£9558	£61	£744	£8470	£842
Helena	£29	£7533	£6407	£723	£3421

a How much prize money did each player win altogether?

b Who won the most?

c How much more did this person win than the next highest earner?

d Tom gave half his money to charity and then spent £2791 on a holiday. How much did he have left?

e Anna gave a third of her total winnings to her sister and one half of the total to charity. How much did she have left?

Let's practise

1 First find approximate totals. Then use a written method to find the exact totals.

a 34·69 and 14   **b** 2·8 and 12·94   **c** 120·1, 53·38 and 0·74

d 14·37 and 9·9   **e** 458·7, 12·07 and 3·6   **f** 8·77, 16·9 and 6·78

Check each answer using subtraction.

Let's solve problems

2 a Choose 3 numbers from the ball and find their total.

b Do this 5 more times.

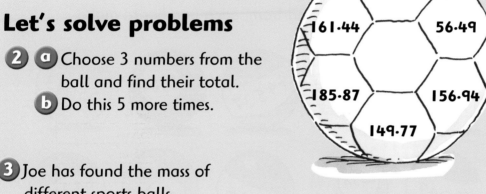

147·0
161·44   56·49
185·87   156·94
149·77

3 Joe has found the mass of different sports balls.

football

482·1 g

table tennis ball

2·53 g

cricket ball

163 g

tennis ball

58·9 g

squash ball

24·6 g

Find the total mass of:

a the football, the tennis ball and the squash ball

b the cricket ball, the table tennis ball and the tennis ball

c all 5 balls.

How much heavier is:

d the football than the squash ball

e the cricket ball than the table tennis ball

f the tennis ball than the table tennis ball?

g Joe carried a bag with 2 footballs, 2 cricket balls and 2 squash balls in it. If the total mass of the balls and the bag was 2 kg, what was the mass of the bag?

Let's practise

1 First find approximate answers.
Then use a written method to find the exact answers.

a 7554 − 2287　　　**b** 8361 − 7458　　　**c** 9904 − 3684

d 8319 − 4356　　　**e** 9223 − 6594　　　**f** 8303 − 5881

Check each answer using addition.

2 Find what has been added to, or subtracted from, each number to make
the next.

a START 3773　37735　4453　44537　5504　FINISH 55043

b 3804 START　38047　8554　85546　6436　FINISH 64369

Let's investigate

3 Abigail used the digits 1 to 9 to make these subtractions.

12 345 − 6789 =

23 456 − 7891 =

34 567 − 8912 =

45 678 − 9123 =

56 789 − 1234 =

a Copy and complete each subtraction. Write about the pattern Abigail used.

b Find the difference between each answer and the previous one.

c Continue the pattern, finding differences between answers.

d Write about any patterns you notice.

Let's practise

1 Use a written method to find the answers.

a 137·5 − 23·32   **b** 572·59 − 59·8   **c** 174·8 − 39·59

d 85·7 − 26·48   **e** 407·6 − 48·68   **f** 430·8 − 95·68

Let's solve problems

2 Here are the diameters of different sports balls.

snooker ball	volleyball	hockey ball	croquet ball	football
5·24 cm	**21·3 cm**	**7·32 cm**	**9·3 cm**	**21·83 cm**

Compare diameters. Which is greater and by how many cm:

a the football or the hockey ball

b the volleyball or the croquet ball

c the hockey ball or the snooker ball

d the volleyball or the hockey ball

e the croquet ball or the snooker ball?

Let's investigate

3 Investigate using these 3 cards to complete
the subtraction below in as many different ways as possible.   5 6 7

9 · 8 − ☐ · ☐ ☐

Find each answer.

Arrange the answers in pairs, each with the same total.

? What if the subtraction was   9 · 8 ☐ − ☐ · ☐ ?

Let's practise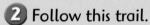

1 Estimate the total of each bill.
What is the difference between your estimate and the exact answer?

a

£6·70
81 p
£7·25
70p
£17·06
£15·34
£25·99

b

£6·99
£13·16
£7·25
55p
£12·25
£3·40
95p

c

£14·70
47p
£8·25
£2·70
£12·06
£7·31
£16·39

Let's investigate

2 Follow this trail.

What number do you end up with?
Investigate for other whole and decimal number starters.

3 Use the 4 numbers ⎡24⎤ ⎡37⎤ ⎡42⎤ ⎡87⎤ to complete this calculation:

$$(\Box + \Box) \times (\Box + \Box) =$$

Investigate finding as many different answers as possible.

? What if the calculation was $(\Box - \Box) \times (\Box - \Box) = ?$

Let's solve problems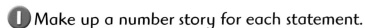

1 Make up a number story for each statement.

  a 254·5 + 38·65 = 293·15
  b 82·4 − 6·79 = 75·61
  c 8·46 × 32 = 270·72
  d 409·36 ÷ 56 = 7·31

2 Six schools were each given 80 free children's tickets to a football match. Each ticket normally cost £5·50.

  a How many pounds' worth of tickets were given away free?

  b If 413 of the free tickets were used at the match, how many were not used?

3 At the match twice as many children paid for a ticket as used a free ticket.

  a How many children paid for a ticket?

  b How many children were there at the match?

  c In the crowd of 6856 adults and children, 253 of the adults were women. How many men were at the match?

4 There were no free tickets for adults. Adults paid £8·00 each.

  a How much money was collected for all the adult tickets?

  b How much money was collected for all the tickets, including those of the children who paid?

5 £5142 was spent on refreshments at the football ground and twice as much was spent on programmes as on refreshments.

  a How much money was raised in total at the ground, including tickets, refreshments and programmes?

  b How much was spent on average (mean) by each person at the ground?

Let's practise

1 Copy each question. Complete it in 2 ways.
Draw loops to show which numbers you multiplied first.

a $12 \times 3 \times 10 =$ ▢   **b** $8 \times 15 \times 5 =$ ▢   **c** $18 \times 4 \times 2.5 =$ ▢

d $14 \times 9 \times 5 =$ ▢   **e** $3.5 \times 14 \times 2 =$ ▢   **f** $15 \times 1.2 \times 5 =$ ▢

2 List any pairs or sets of related calculations.

You may need to think carefully!

8×9	3.5×16	$224 \div (2 \times 4)$
$(4 + 5) \times 8$	$8 \times 3.5 \times 8$	$72 \div 9$
8×28	9×8	$224 \div 8$
$4 \times 9 \times 2$	$2 \times 3.5 \times 8$	$72 \div (4 + 5)$
7×8	$2 \times 2 \times 18$	$2 \times 4 \times 7$

3 The number 3·6 can be written as $9 \times 0.4 = 3.6$ or as $7.2 \div (8 - 6) = 3.6$.

Write 10 calculations using **×** or **÷** (and **+** or **−** if you wish) with the answer:

a 3·6   **b** 84   **c** 12·8

Let's investigate

4 Investigate using these cards to make as many number statements as you can.

| 5 | 0·64 | 0·4 | 8 | 51·2 | 6·4 |

| × | ÷ | = |

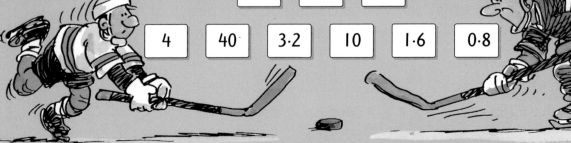

| 4 | 40 | 3·2 | 10 | 1·6 | 0·8 |

Let's practise

1 Copy and complete, using **+**, **−**, **x** or **÷** in each circle.

a (12 ⬤ 3) − (4 ⬤ 5) = 16

b (12 ⬤ 3) ⬤ 45 = 180

c (1 ⬤ 2) ⬤ 34 ⬤ 5 = 22

d (123 ⬤ 4) ⬤ 5 = 595

e 12 ⬤ (3 ⬤ 4) ⬤ 5 = 19

f 123 ⬤ (4 ⬤ 5) = 122·2

2 Use each set of digits to make a number statement, keeping the order of the digits the same.

④ ② ⑨ ⑤ ④ → (4 + 2) × 9 = 54

You can use +, −, ×, ÷, =, but you must use brackets.

a ③ ⑥ ④ ⑤ ④   **b** ⑤ ⑨ ① ④ ⓪   **c** ⑧ ⑤ ③ ⑨

d ⑤ ③ ② ② ⑤   **e** ① ② ⑥ ③ ②   **f** ⑥ ② ⑨ ② ⑦

Let's investigate

3 Tovia used the digits ③ ④ ⑥ and ② in that order, and **+**, **−**, **x**, **÷**, to make 2 different answers.

(3 × 4) − (6 × 2) = 0 and 3 + (4 × 6) ÷ 2 = 13·5

Investigate using the same 4 digits as Tovia to make as many different answers as you can. Keep the order of the digits the same.

? What if the digits were ⑨ ⑧ ⑦ and ⑥ ?

Let's practise

1 Copy and round each decimal to the nearest tenth.

a 1·73　　**b** 2·38　　**c** 5·62　　**d** 7·34

e 3·296　　**f** 4·666　　**g** 12·257　　**h** 16·405

2 Each incomplete number below has been rounded to the nearest tenth.
List all the possible numbers that each one could be.

a [3] [·] [9] [ ] ▶ 3·9　　　　**b** [8] [·] [6] [ ] ▶ 8·7

c [2] [·] [ ] [6] ▶ 2·1　　　　**d** [9] [·] [ ] [ ] ▶ 9·2

e [5] [·] [ ] [ ] ▶ 5·6　　　　**f** [ ] [·] [ ] [ ] ▶ 7·2

Let's investigate 🖩

3 When a 2-digit number is divided by a 1-digit number the answer might be:

| a whole number 20 ÷ 5 = 4 | or | a decimal that stops 15 ÷ 8 = 1·875 | or | a decimal with repeating digits 21 ÷ 9 = 2·333 333... |

Investigate dividing 2-digit numbers by 1-digit numbers.
Draw a table like this to record your findings.

| Division | Answers | | | |
	Whole number	Decimals that stop	Decimals that repeat	Rounded to the nearest tenth
20 ÷ 5	4			4·0
15 ÷ 8		1·875		1·9
21 ÷ 9			2·333 333	2·3

Write about the divisions and how you can predict
which column the answer will be in.

Let's practise

1 Write the answer to each division as an amount of money in pounds.

- **a** £7 ÷ 10
- **b** £13 ÷ 10
- **c** £37 ÷ 100
- **d** £53 ÷ 100
- **e** £9 ÷ 100
- **f** £123 ÷ 100
- **g** £367 ÷ 100
- **h** £501 ÷ 100

Let's solve problems

2 Look at these packs of cassette tapes.

- **a** 4 FOR £7
- **b** 6 FOR £7·50
- **c** 8 FOR £12
- **d** 9 FOR £13·05
- **e** 12 FOR £16·20
- **f** 15 FOR £18·60

Work out the cost of one tape from each pack.
Which pack gives the cheapest price for each tape?

3 Each group of people wins £76·80 on the lottery.
How much will each person in each group get, if the money is shared equally?

a   **b**    **c**    **d**

4

a Eight children spent £94 on CDs. They each spent the same amount. How much did each one spend?

b Fifteen cinema tickets cost £78·75. How much did each one cost?

c Seven people saved £87·92. They each saved the same amount. How much did each one save?

d Eighteen children paid £112·50 to enter the theme park. How much was the entry fee?

Let's solve problems

1 I have 150 books. Each shelf can hold 35 books.
How many shelves do I need?

2 A bus ticket to town is £2·30. I have £10.
How many tickets could I buy?

3 I have 350 photos. I can fit 8 on a page in my album.
How many pages will I need?

4 Dan has £43 to spend on gift vouchers. The vouchers are £5·50 each.
How many can he buy?

5 I have 267 photos. I can fit 14 into a photo frame.
How many frames will I need?

6 I have saved £75. A cinema ticket costs £3·70.
How many times could I go to the cinema?

7 One minibus can carry 14 people.
There are 220 people going on a trip.
How many minibuses are needed?

8 How many 12-cm lengths of string can
I cut from a piece that is 2·75 m long?

9 A bucket holds 9 litres. How many times must I fill it to pour 160
litres of water on my garden?

10 At work I put 5000 sheets of card into trays. A tray holds 750 sheets.
How many trays will I need?

11 Use these numbers to write a question like
the ones above that has an answer of 8.

12 Use these numbers to write a question that
has an answer of 12.

Let's practise

1 Copy and complete.

a 0·6 multiplied by 7 is ☐ **b** eight nine hundreds are ☐

c 7·2 divided by 8 is ☐ **d** 0·8 × 8 is ☐

e 0·7 times 4 is ☐ **f** 1·1 multiplied by 9 is ☐

2 Copy and complete.

a 2 × ☐ = 150 **b** half of ☐ = 290

c double ☐ = 18.8 **d** 1380 divided by 2 = ☐

e 0·54 multiplied by 2 = ☐ **f** ☐ × 980 = 1960

Let's solve problems

3 **a** Twice as many people were in the cinema on Tuesday compared with Monday. There were 870 people on Monday. How many were there on Tuesday?

b Half as much money was spent in Computers-R-Us today compared with yesterday. £17 600 was spent yesterday. How much was spent today?

Let's play A game for 2

You need

a pack of playing cards with the picture cards removed

- Shuffle the cards and place them in a pile face down.
- Player 1 turns over a card. This is the multiplier, the number that player 2 will multiply by.
- Player 1 now turns over 6 cards, one after another.
- Player 2 multiplies each card by the multiplier and says the answers aloud.
- One point is scored for each correct answer.
- Players now swap roles.

The player with more points after five turns each is the winner.

Let's practise

1 Copy and complete these doubling patterns.

a
1 × 9 = ☐
2 × 9 = ☐
4 × 9 = ☐
8 × 9 = ☐
16 × 9 = ☐
32 × 9 = ☐

b
1 × 24 = ☐
2 × 24 = ☐
4 × 24 = ☐
8 × 24 = ☐
16 × 24 = ☐
32 × 24 = ☐

c
1 × 32 = ☐
2 × 32 = ☐
4 × 32 = ☐
8 × 32 = ☐
16 × 32 = ☐
32 × 32 = ☐

Extend each pattern for 2 more doubles.

2 Copy and complete each multiplication.
Show how you halved and doubled to find the answer.

doubled ↓   ↓ halved
$$16 \times 20 = 320$$
$$32 \times 10 = 320$$

a 42 × 20 = ☐
b 45 × 14 = ☐
c 40 × 18 = ☐
d 16 × 33 = ☐
e 21 × 20 = ☐
f 5 × 86 = ☐
g 80 × 25 = ☐
h 8 × 12·5 = ☐
i 160 × 25 = ☐
j 12·5 × 16 = ☐
k 14 × 150 = ☐
l 18 × 500 = ☐

Let's investigate

3 **a** Copy and complete this doubling pattern.

1 × 17 = ☐   2 × 17 = ☐   4 × 17 = ☐   8 × 17 = ☐

Write 5 more doubles for the pattern.

b Eva noticed that she could use 2 × 17 and 16 × 17 to find 18 × 17 like this:

$$18 \times 17 = (2 \times 17) + (16 \times 17)$$
$$= \quad 34 \quad + \quad 272$$
$$= \quad 306$$

Investigate ways of finding other
multiples of 17 from 13 × 17 to 39 × 17,
using the doubling pattern facts.

? What if you worked out the doubling
pattern for multiples of 23?

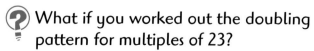

Let's practise

1 Lia found the answer to 24 × 8 like this:

$$24 \times 8 = (20 \times 8) + (4 \times 8)$$
$$= 160 + 32$$
$$= 192$$

Copy and complete.

a 32 × 6 = ▢

b 36 × 5 = ▢

c 38 × 7 = ▢

d 42 × 8 = ▢

e 39 × 8 = ▢

f 54 × 6 = ▢

g 6·7 × 8 = ▢

h 7·6 × 9 = ▢

i 8·7 × 9 = ▢

Let's solve problems

2 Pete and his friends support their football team every weekend. Work out how much they will pay for each trip.

a 6 tickets to Manchester

b 7 tickets to Leeds

c 9 tickets to London

d 5 tickets to Liverpool

e 6 tickets to Middlesbrough

f 8 tickets to Newcastle

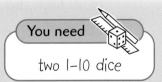

SPECIAL DEALS	
MANCHESTER	£39
LEEDS	£43
MIDDLESBRO'	£87
LIVERPOOL	£74
LONDON	£58
NEWCASTLE	£98

TICKETS

Let's play A game for 2

Each player:

● Rolls a dice and then chooses a shirt.

● Multiplies the number on the shirt by the dice number.

● Records the multiplications and answers.

● Finds how near to 300 they are.

The player nearer to 300 wins 1 point.

The first player to score 5 points is the winner.

You need

two 1–10 dice

29 38 46 58 62 87 94

Let's practise

1
- **a** $4.25 \times 10 = \square$
- **b** $3.8 \times 100 = \square$
- **c** $0.42 \times \square = 42$
- **d** $\square \div 100 = 0.7$
- **e** $54 \div \square = 0.54$
- **f** $\square \times 2 = 1.8$
- **g** $\square \div 2 = 0.75$
- **h** $0.5 \times 8 = \square$
- **i** $49 \times 6 = \square$

2 Use only the numbers and symbols on each bag to write 4 different calculations and their answers.

a

240 ÷
= 80
3 ×

b
100 ÷
× 12.5
8 =

c

0.75 =
× 3
4 ÷

Let's solve problems

3
- **a** Dan's dart landed 93 mm away from the bull's-eye. How many centimetres away was it?
- **b** Jo's dart missed the bull's-eye by 7·4 cm. How many millimetres did it miss by?
- **c** Kirsty threw the javelin 16·4 m. How far is that in centimetres?
- **d** Dev threw the javelin 2117 cm. How many metres did he throw it?
- **e** Ben jumped 0·52 m in the high jump. Debbie jumped twice as high. How high did Debbie jump?
- **f** Luke's first jump was 1·1 m high. His second jump was half as high. What height was his second jump?

Let's investigate

4 Katie used only the digit 4 to make the numbers 0, 1 and 2 like this:

$$4 - 4 = 0 \qquad 44 \div 44 = 1 \qquad (4 + 4) \div 4 = 2$$

Investigate making the numbers 3 to 50 using only the digit 4 and the operations +, −, × and ÷.

? What if you used only the digit 2, 3, 5, 6 ...?

Let's practise

1 **a** $9 \times 2 = \square$
$9 \times 20 = \square$
$90 \times 2 = \square$
$90 \times 20 = \square$

b $7 \times 8 = \square$
$7 \times 80 = \square$
$70 \times 8 = \square$
$70 \times 80 = \square$

c $8 \times 9 = \square$
$8 \times 90 = \square$
$80 \times 9 = \square$
$80 \times 90 = \square$

2 Copy each multiplication.
Write an approximate answer,
then calculate the exact answer.

143×5 is about 150×5, which equals 750.

a $362 \times 4 = \square$

b $507 \times 6 = \square$

c $395 \times 8 = \square$

d $2643 \times 5 = \square$

e $3168 \times 6 = \square$

f $4506 \times 7 = \square$

Let's play A game for 2

Spread out the number cards, face down.

Each player:

- Chooses a number from the rounders bats and takes a number card.
- Records the 2 numbers as a multiplication and writes an estimate for the answer.
- Works out the exact answer and calculates the difference between their estimate and the answer.
- The player nearer to the correct answer for their multiplication wins 1 point.

The first player to score 5 points is the winner.

You need

a set of 3–9 number cards

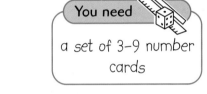
3752
6207

2856

7840
8038
5029

Let's investigate

3 Investigate making as many products as you can to complete this statement:

$\blacksquare \times \blacktriangle = 60\,060$

? What if you found 3 numbers with a product of 60 060?

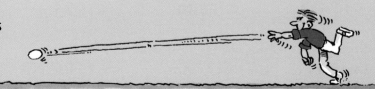

Let's practise

1 Copy and complete.

There are 1·39 euros to £1.

a 139 euros = £ ▢   **b** 13·9 euros = £ ▢

c 13 900 euros = £ ▢   **d** 139 000 euros = £ ▢

e 2·78 euros = £ ▢   **f** ▢ euros = £3

g 278 euros = £ ▢   **h** ▢ euros = £300

Let's play A game for 2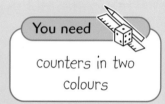

You need

counters in two colours

Use € 1·39 = £1. € means euro

- Each player uses a different colour of counter.
- Player 1 chooses an amount of money on the bag.
- They use a calculator to convert this to euros.
- Player 2 checks the answer.
- If correct, player 1 finds the answer in the grid and covers it with a counter.
- Players swap round.

The first to have 4 counters in a line, vertically, horizontally or diagonally, is the winner.

£40	£58	£80	£3
£10	£24	£44	£90
£75	£22	£11	
£63	£45	£20	£54
£19	£31	£33	£99
£82	£27	£73	£78
£70		£60	

€4·17	€62·55	€37·53	€30·58	€61·16
€80·62	€113·98	€108·42	€137·61	€55·60
€45·87	€111·20	€33·36	€43·09	€83·40
€104·25	€125·10	€15·29	€27·80	€101·47
€13·90	€26·41	€75·06	€97·30	€87·57

Let's practise

1 Copy each multiplication.
Write an approximate answer, then calculate the exact answer.

a 12 × 45 = ▢　　**b** 17 × 36 = ▢　　**c** 28 × 39 = ▢
d 31 × 42 = ▢　　**e** 35 × 45 = ▢　　**f** 38 × 47 = ▢

Let's solve problems

2 Estimate first, then find the exact area of each field.

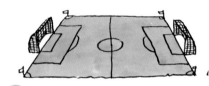

a 165 m long, 32 m wide

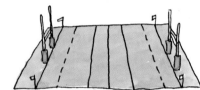

b 146 m long, 42 m wide

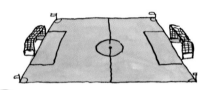

c 216 m long, 34 m wide

d 370 m long, 36 m wide

Let's investigate

3 Shola uses these 5 digit cards to make this 3-digit times 2-digit calculation:

| 4 | 7 | 6 | 3 | 5 |

| 4 | 7 | 6 | × | 3 | 5 |

What is the answer to Shola's calculation?

Investigate making other 3-digit times 2-digit calculations using these digit cards.

Write your multiplications in order of size of answer.
● What is the largest possible answer?
● What is the smallest possible answer?

Is it possible to make a multiplication with an answer of 47 085?

? What if the multiplication was a 2-digit times 3-digit calculation?

Let's practise

1 Dan has been doing this division.

```
237 ÷ 5        237
             - 100        20 × 5
               137
             - 100        20 × 5
                37
             -  35         7 × 5
                 2        47 × 5

answer = 47 2/5
```

Copy and complete using this or another method.

a $169 ÷ 4 =$ ☐   **b** $287 ÷ 4 =$ ☐   **c** $346 ÷ 5 =$ ☐   **d** $384 ÷ 5 =$ ☐

e $593 ÷ 5 =$ ☐   **f** $637 ÷ 4 =$ ☐   **g** $659 ÷ 8 =$ ☐   **h** $719 ÷ 8 =$ ☐

Let's solve problems

2 a Lisa put a total of 134 litres of petrol into her car on five visits to the garage. She put the same amount in each time. How much was this?

b Sam and his three friends have saved £281 between them for a holiday. They share it equally. How much does each get?

c Deepa has used 539 grams of sugar to make eight cakes of equal mass. How much sugar is in each cake?

Let's play   A game for 2

You need

a set of 0–9 digit cards

Spread out the digit cards, face down.

Each player:

● Chooses four cards and makes a 3-digit divided by 1-digit calculation.

● Calculates the answer using a written method and checks using a calculator.

The player whose answer is nearer to 100 scores 1 point.
The first to score 3 points is the winner.

Let's practise

1 **a** $68 \div \square = 17$ **b** $76 \div \square = 8$ **c** $82 \div \square = 4$

   d $75 \div 6 = \square$ **e** $86 \div 8 = \square$ **f** $98 \div 8 = \square$

2 **a** $377 \div 13 = \square$ **b** $416 \div 6 = \square$ **c** $448 \div 32 = \square$

   d $527 \div \square = 17$ **e** $406 \div \square = 14$ **f** $612 \div \square = 18$

   g $\square \div 21 = 18$ **h** $\square \div 14 = 17$ **i** $\square \div 23 = 34$

Let's play   A game for 2

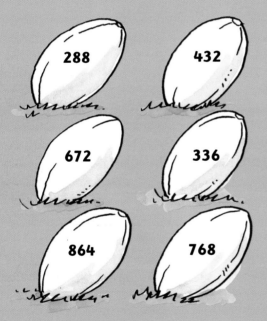

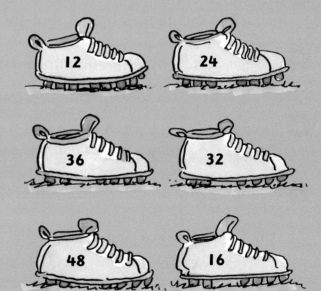

Each player:

● Chooses a number from a ball and a number from a boot.

● Writes a division with the 2 numbers and estimates the answer.

● Finds the correct answer using a written method and checks with a calculator.

The player whose estimate is nearer to their answer scores 1 point.
The first to score 3 points is the winner.

Let's solve problems

1 Find 2 numbers with:

   a a quotient of 3 and a product of 48

   b a sum of 30 and a quotient of 9.

2 There are 87·5 litres of water in 7 fish tanks.
There is the same amount of water in each tank.
How much water is in each tank?

3 In 5 visits to the garage John buys a total of 97·5 litres of petrol for his car.
How much petrol does he buy on average at each visit?

4 Jack thinks of a number. He multiplies it by 9. His answer is 93·6.
What was the number he first thought of?

5 A piece of rope is 57·4 m long and is cut into 7 equal lengths.
How long is each new piece?

6 Jill wrote 81·6 + 6 when she should have written 81·6 ÷ 6.
What is the difference between the answers to the 2 calculations?

7 Eight piles of sand contain a total of 98·4 kg of sand.
All the piles are the same size.
What is the mass of each pile?

8 A shop has 96·6 litres of paraffin in stock. It sells 7 litres a day.
How long does its stock last?

9 Molly thinks of a number. She multiplies it by 8. Her answer is 73·6.
What was the number she first thought of?

10 The same number is missing from these 2 boxes.
The difference between the 2 answers is 75.
What could the missing number be?

        94·5 ÷ ▣

        94·5 − ▣

Let's practise

> A multiple of 5 has a last digit of 0 or 5.
> A multiple of 8 has the last 3 digits divisible by 8.
> A multiple of 9 has the sum of its digits divisible by 9.

Use this information to find which numbers on the trophy are:

a divisible by 5

b divisible by 8

c divisible by 9.

Make a list of each set of numbers.

On the trophy: 88   117   405   4120   2835   1224   8640   5672   3681

Let's play   A game for 2

You need
counters in 2 colours

● Take turns to choose a number and a factor from the grids.

● Check that each other's number is divisible by the factor.

● If it is, the player who chose the number and factor covers each of them with a counter. These numbers can no longer be used.

The first player to cover 5 factors is the winner.

Numbers

126	171	675	360	500	54	175
300	135	252	225	140	170	64
780	884	270	666	325	42	700

Player 1's factors

2	3	4	5	6	8	9	10	25	100

Player 2's factors

2	3	4	5	6	8	9	10	25	100

Let's practise

1 Write how far each child cycled in kilometres.

a 7216 m   **b** 7012 m   **c** 7602 m   **d** 7610 m   **e** 7006 m

2 Write how far each person ran in metres.

a 3·457 km   **b** 2·8 km   **c** 3·39 km   **d** 4·08 km   **e** 5·605 km   **f** 0·97 km

Let's solve problems

3 Each practice ground is rectangular. The width of each is half its length. Find the width and perimeter of each practice ground.

a length 70 m   **b** length 48 m   **c** length 27 m   **d** length 35 m

4 Look at the table. What is:

Description	Length
length of race	10 000 m
distance to sports club	1000 m
length of sprint	100 m
width of running track	10 m
height of hurdle	1 m
water depth in steeplechase pool	0·1 m
width of lines of running track	0·01 m
thickness of gold medal	0·001 m

a $\frac{1}{100}$ of the width of the running track

b 1000 times the thickness of a gold medal

c the area of paint on one line of the 100 m running track?

d What fraction of the 10 000 m race is:
- the distance to the sports club
- the height of 10 hurdles?

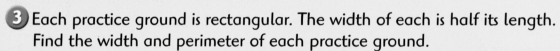

Let's practise

① Use the scale to find the diameter of each medal to the nearest millimetre.
Write each diameter in mm and in cm.

bronze

silver

gold

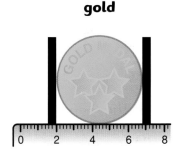

Let's solve problems

② If medals from question **1** are
placed end to end, what is the
approximate total length
in metres of:

ⓐ 100 gold medals   **ⓑ** 1000 silver medals   **ⓒ** 10 000 bronze medals?

③ If bronze medals are placed to form a
straight line, how many make 1 kilometre?

Use a calculator

④ Each medal is on 30 inches of ribbon.

ⓐ How many medals will use 75 m of ribbon?

ⓑ How many metres of ribbon are needed for:

● 500 medals   ● 2000 medals?

1 inch ≈ 2·5 cm

⑤ Each medal is 4 mm thick.

ⓐ How many metres high is a stack of 100 medals?

ⓑ How many medals are in a stack 1 m high?

Let's practise

1 Write the mass of each newborn baby in kilograms.

a 3605 g　　　**b** 3090 g　　　**c** 2840 g

d 3450 g　　　**e** 4540 g　　　**f** 4125 g

Let's solve problems

2 At the 4-month check-up, each baby in question 1 has doubled its birth mass. Write each new mass to the nearest $\frac{1}{10}$ kg.

3 This table shows Ben's mass at different ages.

Age in years	2	4	6	8	10	12	14	16	18
Mass in kg	13·1	15·9	20·8	23·7	29·2	35·6	47·5	57·3	64·4

a Write each mass in grams.

b Between which ages did he gain the least mass? Write his mass gain in grams.

c Between which ages did he gain the most mass? Write his mass gain in grams.

4 Lisa, Mary and Nina are 3 friends. Together their mass is exactly 100 kg. Lisa is 800 g lighter than Mary. Mary is 0·6 kg lighter than Nina. What is the mass of each girl? Explain how you worked it out.

Let's practise

$$2\frac{1}{4}\,lb \approx 1\,kg$$

1 Write the mass each scale shows, in lb and kg.

a

b

c

☐ lb ≈ ☐ kg   ☐ lb ≈ ☐ kg   ☐ lb ≈ ☐ kg

2 Use the conversion scale to work out these masses.
Round your answers to the nearest 10 grams or to the nearest $\frac{1}{4}$ lb.

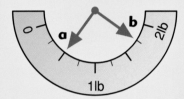

a ☐ lb ≈ ☐ g   **b** ☐ lb ≈ ☐ g

c ☐ g ≈ ☐ lb   **d** ☐ g ≈ ☐ lb

Let's solve problems

3 Write the mass of the food in metric units.
Round your answers to the nearest 10 g.

a 2 lb   **b** $1\frac{1}{4}$ lb   **c** $\frac{3}{4}$ lb

4 Write the mass of each food item in imperial units.
Round your answers to the nearest $\frac{1}{4}$ lb.

a 2 eggs   **b** 8 sausages
   120 g   454 g

5 A recipe for 'Toad in the hole' needs 10 eggs and 12 sausages.
Work out the total mass of eggs and sausages in metric and imperial units.

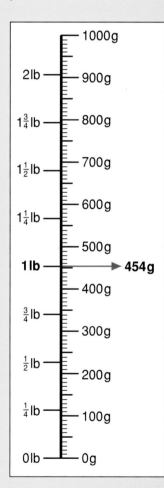

2lb	1000g
	900g
$1\frac{3}{4}$ lb	800g
$1\frac{1}{2}$ lb	700g
$1\frac{1}{4}$ lb	600g
1lb	500g
	454g
	400g
$\frac{3}{4}$ lb	300g
$\frac{1}{2}$ lb	200g
$\frac{1}{4}$ lb	100g
0lb	0g

Let's solve problems

Animal	Average body mass		Average mass of food at each meal	
	lb	kg	lb	kg
elephant	9020	4100	400	180
polar bear	1500	680	150	68
tiger	500	227	77	35

1 Write the mass of the elephant, polar bear and tiger in tonnes.

> 1000 kg = 1 tonne

2 **a** What percentage of its body mass does a polar bear eat at each meal?

b To get enough energy, a polar bear must eat once about every 6 days. Work out the average mass of food per day in lb and in kg.

3 A tiger needs to eat about 14 lb or 6·4 kg of food for a day's worth of energy. About how many days can it leave between meals?

4 Look at this table. What percentage of its body mass does:

a a vampire bat eat at each meal

b a hamster eat at each meal?

Animal	Average body mass		Average mass of food at each meal	
	oz	g	oz	g
vampire bat	1	28	1	28
hamster	3·6	100	0·36	10

5 A queen bee lays about 2000 eggs a day.
She needs to eat 80 times her body mass each day to stay alive.
The average mass of a queen bee is 0·112 g.
Find the mass of food she must eat each day to the nearest gram.
Show all your working.

Let's solve problems

1 20 cl of water is poured into each measuring jug.
Write the new level in millilitres.

| 100 ml = 10 cl = 0·1 l |

a

b

c

2 Write the capacity of each drinks
container in centilitres, then in litres.

d
e
f

a 250 ml   **b** 750 ml   **c** 330 ml   1500 ml   500 ml   870 ml

3

SPECIAL OFFERS

any 3 for the price of 2   **50% extra free**

a What is the total number of litres shown in each special offer?

b Mrs Rossi buys 1 carton of orange juice and 1 carton of apple juice on special
offer, and 3 bottles of energy drink for her children's Sports Day.
How many litres of drink does she get altogether?

Let's solve problems

Use the conversion graph to help you with these questions.

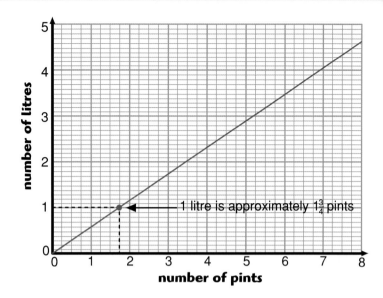

number of litres

1 litre is approximately $1\frac{3}{4}$ pints

number of pints

① Write how many litres, to the nearest $\frac{1}{10}$ of a litre, each bottle holds.

ⓐ 2 pints   **ⓑ** 5 pints   **ⓒ** 8 pints

ⓓ $\frac{1}{2}$ pint   **ⓔ** $10\frac{1}{2}$ pints   **ⓕ** $13\frac{1}{2}$ pints

② Approximately how many pints, to the nearest $\frac{1}{2}$ pint, are in:

ⓐ 4 litres   **ⓑ** 7 litres   **ⓒ** 9 litres   **ⓓ** 1·7 litres   **ⓔ** 4·2 litres?

③ What percentage of the larger measure is the smaller measure?

		ⓐ	ⓑ	ⓒ	ⓓ	ⓔ	ⓕ
Capacity of bucket		4 pints	4 pints	6 pints	8 pints	8 pints	2 pints
Capacity of watering can		1 gallon	2 gallons	1 gallon	10 gallons	5 gallons	5 gallons

45 l

④ What is the approximate capacity of the water butt

ⓐ in gallons   **ⓑ** in pints?

Let's solve problems

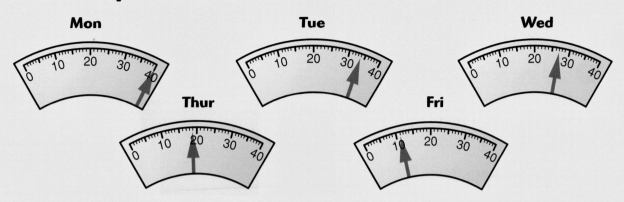

Mon   **Tue**   **Wed**   **Thur**   **Fri**

1) The gauges show the litres of petrol in Harry's mum's car at the start of each school day. She begins the week with a full tank of petrol. Write the amount of petrol at the start of each school day.

2) How many litres of petrol did Harry's mum use on Monday?

3) On which days did she use 20% of the fuel capacity of her car?

Use this scale to help you answer questions 4 and 5 below.

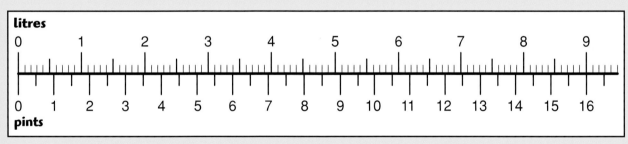

litres
0   1   2   3   4   5   6   7   8   9

pints
0 1 2 3 4 5 6 7 8 9 10 11 12 13 14 15 16

4) On Saturday morning there are 2 gallons of petrol left in the tank.

   a) How many litres did Harry's mum use on Friday?

   b) She fills the tank at the petrol station. How many litres does she buy?

5) Harry washes the car on Sunday. He uses $4\frac{1}{2}$ buckets of water. Work out how much water he uses:

   a) in litres   b) in gallons   c) in pints.

Let's solve problems

1 Two rectangles have been joined to make 4 different shapes.

    a Find the perimeter of each shape in grid units.
Each side of a small square on the grid is 1 unit long.

    b Write the perimeters in order.

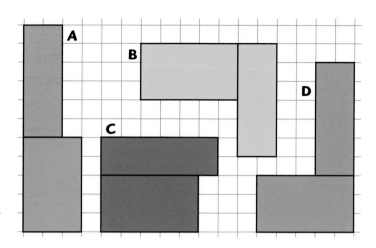

2 These shapes are made with regular polygons.
The small equilateral triangle has a perimeter of 6 cm.
Find the perimeter of each shape.

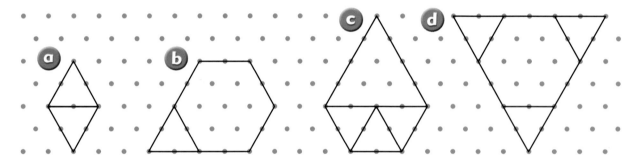

Let's investigate

3 These triangles are isosceles.
Their equal sides are twice as long as their base.

    a Copy and complete the table.

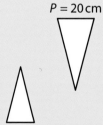 $P = 10\,cm$

 $P = 20\,cm$ $P = 30\,cm$

 $P = 40\,cm$

 $P = 50\,cm$

Perimeter of triangle in cm	10	20	30	40	50	60	70
Length of base in cm	2						

    b If *P* represents the perimeter and *L* the length of the base, write a formula relating *P* and *L*.

    c Use your formula to find the length of the base when the perimeter is 100 cm.

Let's solve problems

1 Use the formula $A = l \times b$ to calculate the area of each wall tile.

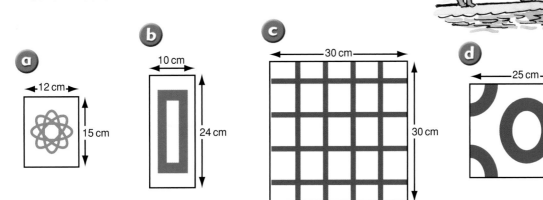

a
12 cm
15 cm

b
10 cm
24 cm

c
30 cm
30 cm

d
25 cm
20 cm

2 Gavin needs to tile a rectangular area 1·5 m by 1·2 m.

- How many of the tiles from question **1a** does he need?
- Repeat for the other tiles in question **1**.

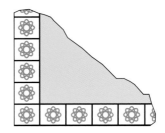

3 Find the area of each cut tile.

Use the chalk marks to help you.

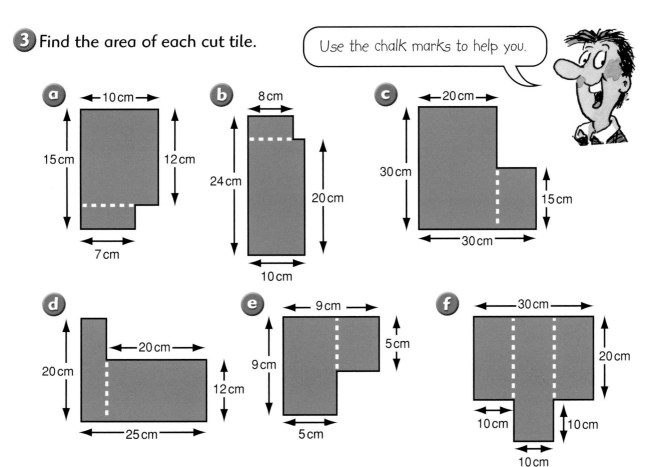

a
10 cm
15 cm
12 cm
7 cm

b
8 cm
24 cm
20 cm
10 cm

c
20 cm
30 cm
30 cm
15 cm

d
20 cm
20 cm
12 cm
25 cm

e
9 cm
9 cm
5 cm
5 cm
5 cm

f
30 cm
20 cm
10 cm
10 cm
10 cm

Let's solve problems

1 The area and length of 1 side of a rectangle are given.
Find the length of the missing side.

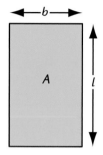

a $A = 54\,m^2$
$b = 6\,m$
$l = ?$

b $A = 240\,cm^2$
$l = 40\,cm$
$b = ?$

c $A = 450\,cm^2$
$l = 30\,cm$
$b = ?$

d $A = 7500\,mm^2$
$l = 250\,mm$
$b = ?$

2 Each shape was made using 2 squares. Write the length of each marked side.

a $X = 100\,m^2$
$Y = 25\,m^2$

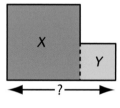

b $X = 64\,m^2$
$Y = 16\,m^2$

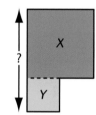

c $X = 81\,m^2$
$Y = 25\,m^2$

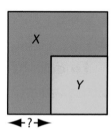

3 **a** Work out the area of the coloured shape below in 3 different ways.

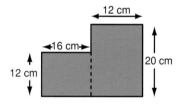

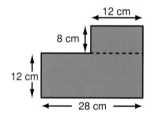

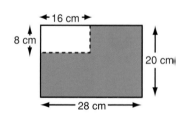

b What do you notice about your answers? Explain why.

Let's investigate

You need

1 cm squared paper

4 Len uses a closed loop of rope 24 m long,
4 pegs and a mallet to mark out
a rectangular area in his garden.
What are the dimensions
of the rectangle that will give him
the largest possible area?

? What if he had a length of rope: **a** 30 m long   **b** 18 m long?

Let's solve problems

You need

Activity Sheet 42

1 It is 12:00 GMT at the prime meridian in London.
What time is it in:

a Oslo   b Beijing

c Chicago   d Hawaii

e Johannesburg   f Sydney?

2 Look at your world map.
Name a city that is:

a 2 hours ahead of London

b 6 hours behind London

c 9 hours ahead of London

d 8 hours behind London.

3 It is 3:30 pm local time in Oslo. Write the time in:

a Perth   b Tokyo   c Mexico City   d Rio de Janeiro.

4 It is 11:15 am in Mexico City.
Write the local time in:

a New York   b Denver

c Chicago   d Vancouver.

5 The daily British Planeways flight from London Gatwick to Houston, Texas
departs at 10:00 and arrives at 14:20 local time.
Houston is 6 hours behind London.
How long is the flight in hours and minutes?

6 The British Planeways flight from Houston to London takes
8 hours and 50 minutes.
It departs from Houston at 4:25 pm local time.
At what time will it land at London Gatwick the next day?

Let's solve problems

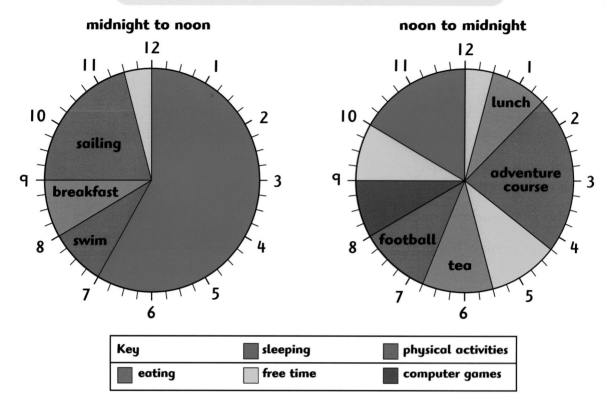

Simon's timetable – Spotlight Summer Camp

midnight to noon

noon to midnight

sailing

breakfast

swim

lunch

adventure course

football

tea

Key		sleeping		physical activities
	eating		free time	computer games

1 Work out how long Simon spent:

a sleeping **b** eating **c** on physical activities **d** with free time.

2 What was Simon doing at:

a 01:15 **b** 11:00 **c** 15:30 **d** 19:45?

3 Write your answers in 24-hour clock notation. Suggest a suitable time when Simon might:

a watch TV **b** write postcards

c visit the shops **d** learn to scuba dive **e** go skateboarding.

4 How much longer does Simon spend on the adventure course than:

a sailing **b** playing football **c** swimming **d** eating breakfast?

Let's practise

1 Look at the 3-D shapes.

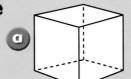 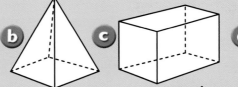

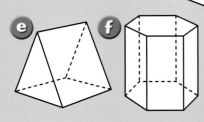 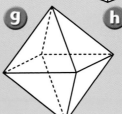 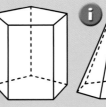 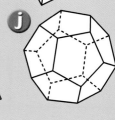

Copy the table and complete it with the letters of the shapes.

	No right-angled faces	1 right-angled face	More than 1 right-angled face
3 edges at each vertex			a
More than 3 edges at 1 or more vertices			

2 **a** These 2 shapes are placed on a horizontal surface. Copy and complete the table.

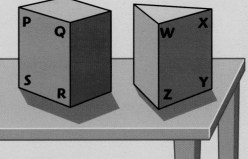

cuboid   triangular prism

3-D shape	Number of			
	horizontal		vertical	
	faces	edges	faces	edges
cuboid				
triangular prism				

b Copy and complete each statement using the word 'parallel' or 'perpendicular'.

● PQ is _____ to RS   ● SP is _____ to SR

● YZ is _____ to WZ   ● XY is _____ to WZ

Let's investigate

3 Plato investigated 3-D shapes.
He found only five 3-D shapes that had:

● faces that are regular polygons

● all faces are congruent (identical)

● the same number of edges meeting at each vertex.

Investigate which five 3-D shapes he found.

Four of the 3-D shapes I found are on this page.

Plato
427–347 BCE

Let's solve problems

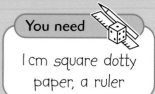
You need

I cm square dotty paper, a ruler

1 ● Copy these quadrilaterals on to 1 cm square dotty paper.

● Draw the next 2 shapes in each sequence.

● Write the name of each shape.

● Draw any lines of symmetry on each shape.

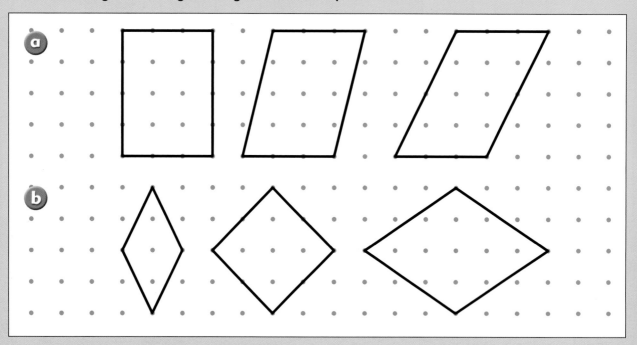

c Copy the table. Use what you did in parts **a** and **b** to help you complete it.

Property of quadrilateral	square	non-square rectangle	non-square rhombus	non-rectangular parallelogram
all sides equal	✓			
opposite sides equal				
opposite sides parallel				
all angles right angles				
opposite angles equal				
no lines of symmetry				
fewer than 4 lines of symmetry				
4 lines of symmetry				

2 Copy these statements. Use your table to complete them.

A parallelogram has its opposite sides _____ and _____ .

A _____ is a parallelogram with 4 equal sides and 2 lines of symmetry.

Let's solve problems

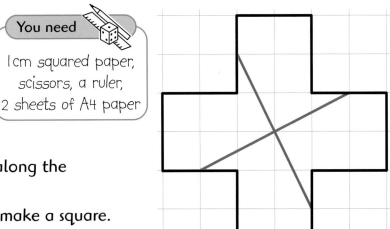

You need

1 cm squared paper, scissors, a ruler, 2 sheets of A4 paper

1. ● Draw this shape on 1 cm squared paper.
   ● Draw the red lines on the cross.
   ● Cut the shape out and cut along the blue lines.
   ● Fit the 4 pieces together to make a square.

Let's investigate

2. ● Make a square from A4 paper.

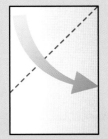 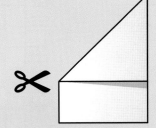 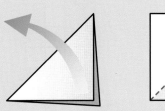

● Find the midpoint of one side and rule these lines on the square.

● Label the shapes A, B and C. Cut them out.

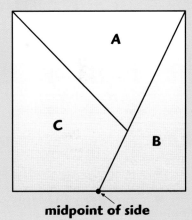

midpoint of side

(a) Karen made a parallelogram and a right-angled triangle with the 3 shapes. Try to do this.

(b) Use the 3 shapes to make different polygons. Draw each polygon, showing how you made it. Name each polygon.

3. ● Make another square from A4 paper.

● Find the midpoints, rule the lines and label the shapes P to T.

● Cut them out.

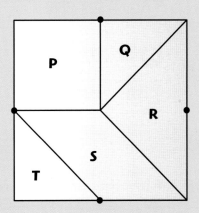

(a) Jacob used shape Q and 2 other shapes to make a square. Try to do this.

(b) Investigate making different polygons using any 3 shapes. Draw and name your polygons, showing how you made each one.

Let's investigate

1 These shapes are hexominoes.

- Make each shape with interlocking square tiles.
- Investigate which shapes are nets of a cube.
- Copy and complete the table.

Hexomino	Net of a cube?	
	Yes	No
a	✓	
b		

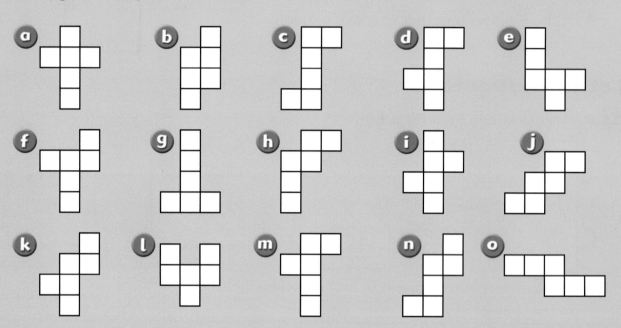

2
- Copy the 3 nets below on to 2 cm squared paper.
- Put a tab on every alternate edge.
- Complete the dots so that opposite faces add up to 7.
- Make the dice.

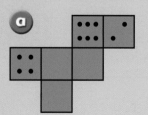

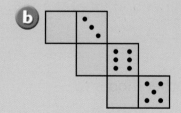

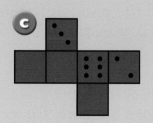

- Investigate making other nets into dice.

Let's solve problems

You need

about 60 interlocking cubes in 2 colours

1 ● Build each shape below with cubes of the same colour.

● Predict the smallest number of extra cubes you will need to make the shape into a cuboid.

● Check by adding the cubes in the second colour.

      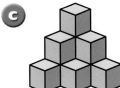

2 ● Build each shape below with interlocking cubes of the same colour.

● Predict the smallest number of extra cubes you will need to cover the ends of the shape (faces coloured green) and join them up.

● Check by adding cubes in the second colour.

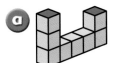 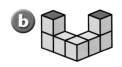 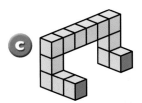

Let's investigate

3 These are skeletal cubes.

a Build each skeletal cube.

b Make the next one in the pattern.

3 x 3 x 3

4 x 4 x 4

c Copy and complete the table.

Skeletal cube	Number of cubes
3 × 3 × 3	
4 × 4 × 4	
5 × 5 × 5	
6 × 6 × 6	

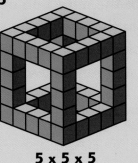

5 x 5 x 5

d Investigate patterns in the table. Write about the patterns you find.

e Predict the number of cubes for a 7 × 7 × 7 skeletal cube.

Let's solve problems

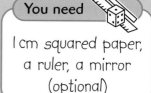

1 **a** Find the number of lines of symmetry for
these regular polygons.
Record your answers in a table like the
one below.

Number of equal sides	3	4	5	6	7	8	10	12	20
Number of lines of symmetry	3								

b Complete the table by predicting the number of lines of symmetry for
regular polygons with 10 sides, 12 sides and 20 sides.

2 S represents the number of sides of a regular polygon.
L represents the number of its lines of symmetry.

a Write a formula to show the relationship between S and L.

b Check that your formula works for regular heptagons and decagons.

Let's investigate

3 A line crosses each polygon.
Investigate the reflection of each
polygon in the line.
Copy each polygon on to 1 cm
squared paper and draw the reflection.

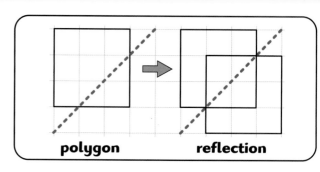

polygon   **reflection**

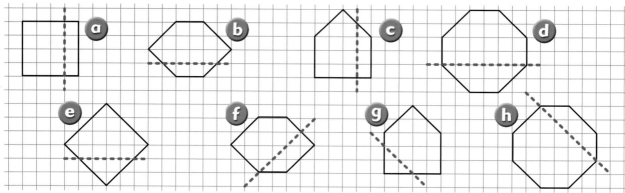

Let's practise

1 Copy each shape, with its axes, on to squared paper. Draw the reflection in the y-axis. List the coordinates of the reflected shape.

You need

1 cm squared paper, a ruler

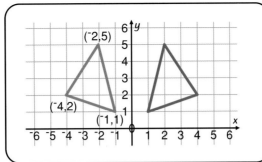

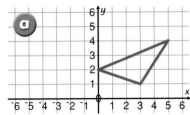

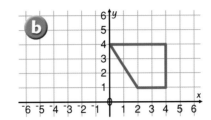

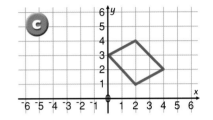

Let's solve problems

2 Copy each shape below onto Activity Sheet 50. Use the x-axis and y-axis as mirror lines and draw the reflections of each shape.

You need

Activity Sheet 50, a ruler

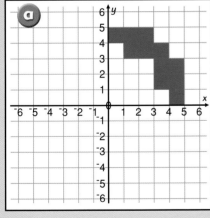

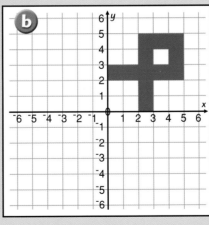

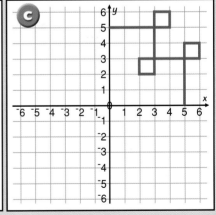

3 a Copy this shape on to Activity Sheet 50.

  b Draw the reflection in the x-axis.

  c Copy and complete the table for the points P, Q and R reflected into all 4 quadrants.

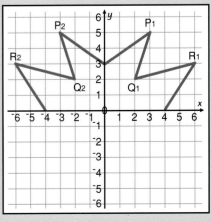

1st quadrant	2nd quadrant	3rd quadrant	4th quadrant
$P_1 = (3, 5)$	$P_2 = (^-3, 5)$	$P_3 =$	$P_4 =$
$Q_1 = (2, 2)$	$Q_2 =$	$Q_3 =$	$Q_4 =$
$R_1 = (6, 3)$	$R_2 =$	$R_3 =$	$R_4 =$

Let's solve problems

1 a Write the coordinates of fielders A to H.

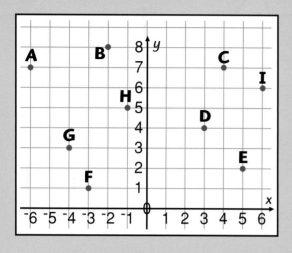

b The batsman is at the point (1, 1). Decide where to position the bowler (O) and the umpire (U). Write their coordinates.

2 Pete's team and Linda's team have a penalty shoot-out.

Rules

- If the coordinates are covered by the keeper, the shot is saved.
- All other coordinates score a goal.

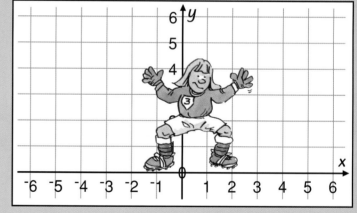

a Copy and complete these scoresheets.

Pete's team

Coordinates of shot	(⁻4, 5)	(2, 3)	(5, 6)	(1, 3)	(5, 1)	(⁻3, 4)	(⁻2, 3)
Result	goal						

Linda's team

Coordinates of shot	(1, 4)	(⁻3, 3)	(6, 5)	(⁻2, 1)	(0, 3)	(⁻6, 3)	(⁻1, 3)
Result	saved						

b Which team won? **c** What was the score?

Let's solve problems

1 Where on the adventure course are these children?

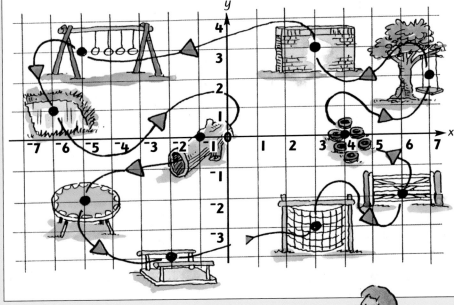

(7,2)

Jason

(⁻5,⁻2)

Paul

(3,⁻3)

Theo

(⁻5,3)

Claire

(4,0)

Jan

2 Write the coordinates of these obstacles.

  a trampoline   **b** wall   **c** rings   **d** gate   **e** tyres

3 Find the position of these children. Write their coordinates.

  a Kenny is at the obstacle ahead of Claire.

  b Ricky is at the obstacle behind Theo.

  c Mandy is at the obstacle after the tree swing.

4 **a** Mrs Siddiqui is at (⁻5, 3). Which obstacle is she supervising?

  b She walks 7 units to the right and 6 units down.
    Write the coordinates of her new position.

  c She then moves on to check the tree swing. Describe her route.

Let's practise

① Look at the course sailed by a yacht.
Estimate each angle to the nearest degree.
Then measure each angle to the nearest degree.

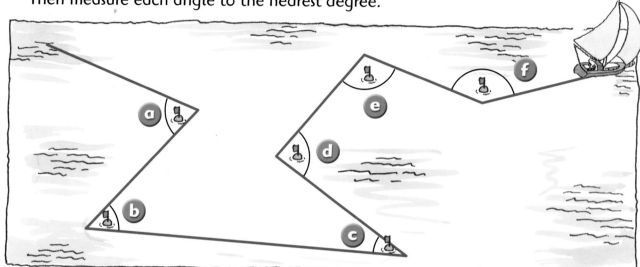

Let's solve problems

② These lines show where the wakes of 2 water-skiers cross.
Calculate the other angles.

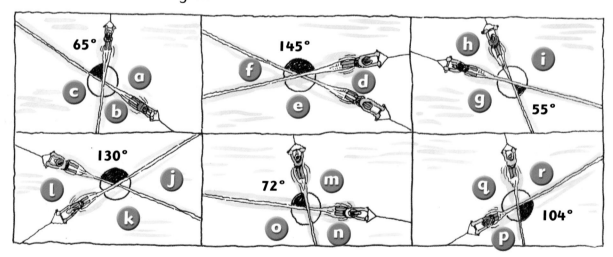

Let's investigate

③ Two power boats are on a parallel course.
Their course is crossed by a jet-skier.
Investigate the sizes of the angles.

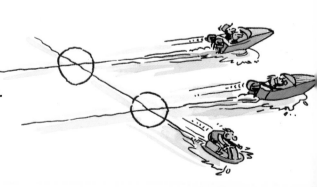

Let's practise

1. **a** Draw 3 large right-angled scalene triangles.

   b Measure the acute angles.

   c What is the sum of each pair of acute angles?

2. Calculate the size of each green angle. Then check by measuring.

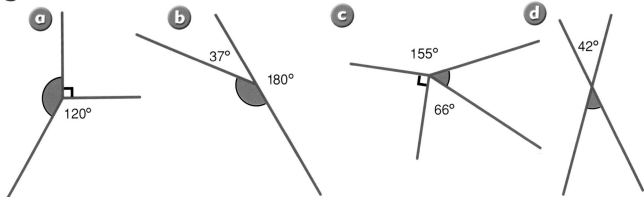

a 120°   **b** 37° 180°   **c** 155° 66°   **d** 42°

Let's investigate

3. ● Draw a diagram like this one.
   ● Measure angles A, B and C to the nearest degree.
   ● Find the sum of angles A, B and C.
   ● Investigate the sum of 3 or more angles on a straight line.

4. **a** Measure the angles in these trapeziums.

   b Find the angle total for each trapezium.

   c Investigate the sum of angles
   in other trapeziums.

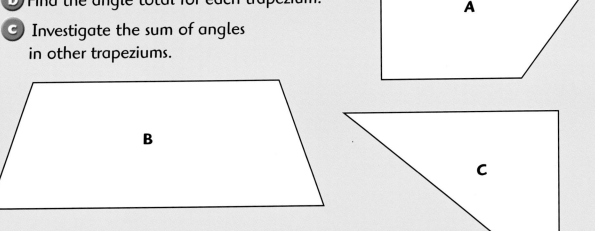

A

B

C

Let's solve problems

1 Copy each statement.
Write whether the 2 possible outcomes
are equally likely or not.
Explain your decision.

    a A new baby will be a boy or a girl.

    b Someone will be left-handed or
       right-handed.

    c A number rolled on a dice will be
       less than 2 or greater than 2.

    d A number rolled on a dice will be
       odd or even.

    e If I drop a slice of buttered toast, it will land butter side
       down or plain side down.

    f A playing card taken from a full pack will be red or black.

Let's investigate

2 **a** Draw a picture on one side of a piece of paper.
       Hold the paper as high as you can with the picture facing outwards.
       Drop it.
       Record the side it lands on.
       Do this 20 times.
       Write about the results.

    b Drop the paper another 20 times.
       Write about these results.
       Compare them with the results
       of the previous 20 drops.

    c Do it again another 20 times.
       Write about these results.
       Compare this set of 20 drops
       with both the previous 20 drops.

    d Combine the three lots of 20 drops
       for a total of 60 drops.
       Write about what you notice.

Let's play   A game for 2

You need
a dice each

● Each player chooses an outcome for their dice
  from this list and records their choice.

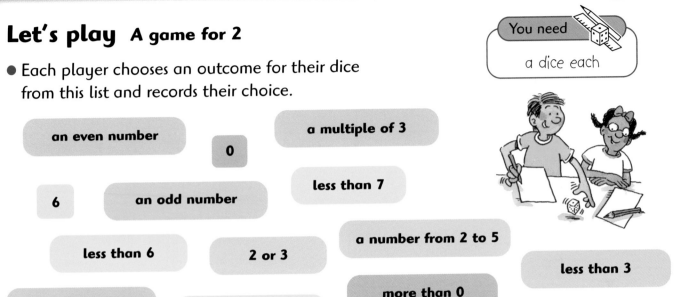

an even number

0

a multiple of 3

6   an odd number   less than 7

less than 6   2 or 3   a number from 2 to 5   less than 3

has a factor of 2   more than 3   more than 0

● Each player rolls their dice.

● A point is scored if the number satisfies the chosen outcome.

● The winner is the first to reach 5 points.

● Play again using different choices of outcome.

Let's investigate

1 Copy this probability scale.

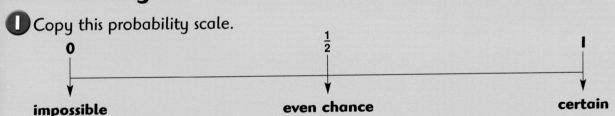

0                    $\frac{1}{2}$ 1

impossible   even chance   certain

Think about the probability of each outcome listed in the game above.
Draw an arrow on the scale in the position you would expect for each outcome.

2 ● Make a table of the outcomes listed in the game.

● Roll the dice 36 times and tally the
  frequency of each outcome.

● Investigate the frequencies. Do they match
  what you expected? Explain your reasoning.

Outcome	Tally
an odd number	
6	
less than 6	

? What if you tally the frequencies of the sum of the numbers on 2 dice?

Let's practise

1 Copy this probability scale.

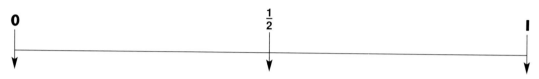

0       $\frac{1}{2}$ 1

Write these words in the correct position on the scale.

| certain | good chance | impossible | even chance | poor chance |

Let's investigate

You need

a pack of playing cards with the picture cards removed

2 Investigate the probabilities of taking different kinds of cards from the pack.

a Predict and record on a probability scale the probability of taking from the pack:
- a black card
- a diamond
- an odd number.

hearts   diamonds   clubs   spades

b Copy the table and continue it to 20.

c Shuffle the cards. Turn over the top card and record it in the table. Do this 20 times.

	Outcome		
	colour	suit	number
1			
2			
3			

d Use a different colour to mark on your probability scale the experimental probabilities of turning over:
- a black card
- a diamond
- an odd number.

e Write about the accuracy of your predictions.

? What if you were interested in these outcomes:
- a red card
- a spade
- an even number?

Let's solve problems

1 A bag contains a total of 12 cubes in 2 colours. How many red cubes and how many blue are in the bag if:

a the probability of choosing a blue is $\frac{1}{3}$

b there is an even chance of choosing a red

c the probability of choosing a red is $\frac{3}{4}$

d it is impossible to choose a red

e it is certain that the choice will be a blue?

Let's investigate

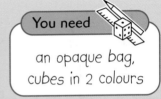

You need

an opaque bag, cubes in 2 colours

2 Work with a partner.

- Player 1 secretly puts some of each colour cube into the bag so there are 12 cubes altogether.

- Player 2 takes out 1 cube, records the colour, and then puts it back.

- Player 2 repeats this 23 more times, shaking the bag between each try.

- Player 2 then guesses how many of each colour are in the bag by:
    ◆ calculating the probability for each colour being chosen
    ◆ recording it as a fraction.

- Player 1 writes about how successful player 2 was in guessing the number of each colour.

- Do this twice each.

? What if you used three colours of cube to make a total of 12?

Let's practise

1 Write as a fraction the probability of scoring a 2 on each of these spinners.

a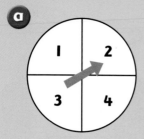

b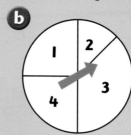

c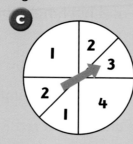

d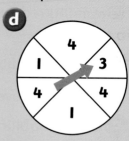

e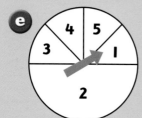

f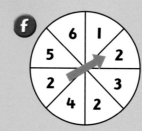

g

h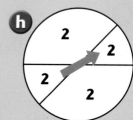

Let's solve problems

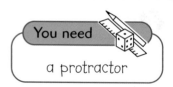
You need
a protractor

2 Design 2 different circular spinners for each probability.
Use a protractor to help you.

a The probability of scoring a 4 is $\frac{3}{4}$.

b The probability of scoring a 1 is $\frac{1}{2}$.

c The probability of scoring a 2 is $\frac{3}{8}$.

d The probability of scoring a 5 is 0.

Let's investigate

3 Draw several copies of this spinner.

a Investigate writing the numbers 1, 2
and 3 on the spinners in different places.

b Write the probability of scoring a 1, a 2
and a 3 on each spinner.

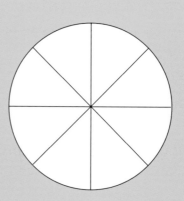

? What if you used the numbers 1, 2, 3 and 4?

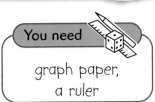
Let's solve problems

This graph shows the temperature in a classroom during one day.
The temperature was taken each hour.
The broken line - - - - shows what the minimum temperature
should be when the children are in school.

You need

graph paper,
a ruler

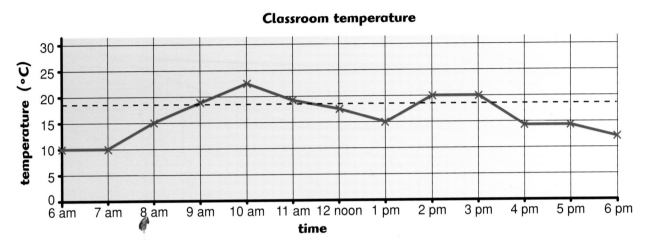

Classroom temperature

1. Work with a partner.
   Discuss the graph.
   Write at least 5 sentences to explain what the graph tells you.
   Use these words to help:

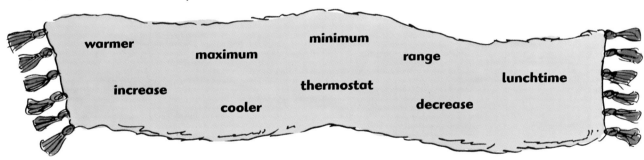

warmer   minimum
        maximum   range
increase   thermostat   lunchtime
        cooler   decrease

2. **a** Draw a line graph about temperature that shows:
   - a maximum of 26 °C and a minimum of 15 °C
   - the temperature above 19 °C
     for all the hours that children
     are in school.

   b How realistic is your graph?

Let's solve problems

1 Use the conversion graph below to convert these amounts to pounds sterling (£).

a €135   **b** €30   **c** €80   **d** €105

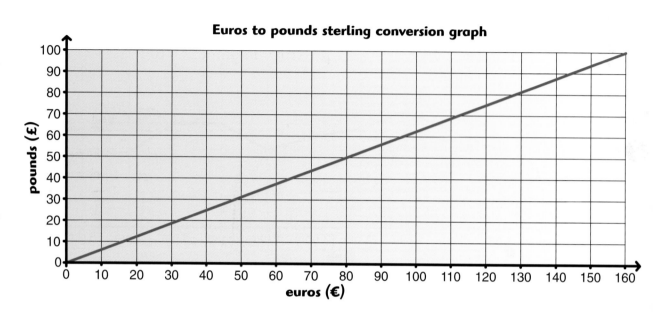

Euros to pounds sterling conversion graph

pounds (£) / euros (€)

2 Use the graph above to price these items in euros (€).

a £55   **b** £25   **c** £80

3 ● Choose 5 items that you might buy.

● Use the graph to find out their price in euros.

● Record each price both in pounds sterling and in euros.

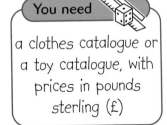

You need

a clothes catalogue or a toy catalogue, with prices in pounds sterling (£)

Let's practise

1 Each set of numbers needs to be grouped for a bar chart.
Write down the groups.
1–30 in groups of 5 → 1–5, 6–10, 11–15, 16–20, 21–25, 26–30

a 0–99 in groups of 10

b 0–24 in groups of 5

c 1–300 in groups of 50

d 1–1000 in groups of 100

Let's investigate

2 Maia says:

There is more football on television than any other sport.

You need

television listings for sports channels

Work with a partner to find out if Maia is correct.

a Look through the schedule of sports programmes for 1 day.
Make a list of all the sports you recognise.

b Record how many times each sport is shown.

c Which sports are on most often?
Make a list of 5 or 6.

d Use your list of sports in part **c**.
Work out approximately how many hours of each sport are shown.

e Is Maia correct?
Write a report of your findings.
Find ways to present your information clearly.

? What if you looked at the television listings for a different day?

Let's practise

1 Estimate the fraction of each circle that is red and the fraction that is blue.

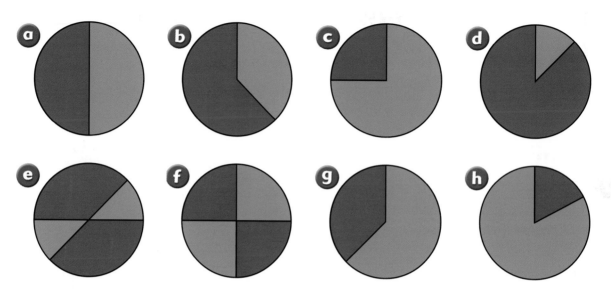

Let's solve problems

2 In Hill Street School there are 48 children in Year 5. This pie chart shows the proportion of children that favour each sport.

Work out how many children favour each sport.

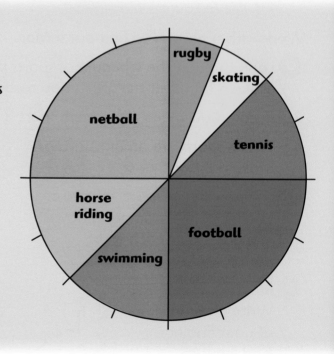

Let's investigate

3 Carry out a survey of 18 children's favourite sports. Use the information to make a pie chart.

You need

a protractor

? What if you conducted a survey of a different group of 18 children?

Let's practise

1 Write the difference between these pairs of numbers.

a 36 and 12   **b** 58 and 136   **c** 47 and 157

d 68 and 35   **e** 77 and 106   **f** 231 and 179

Write the number that is half way between each pair of numbers.

Let's solve problems

2 Find and record the range and mode for these sets of data.

> The <u>range</u> of a set of data is found by finding the difference between the lowest and the highest numbers.
> The <u>mode</u> of a set is the one that appears most often.

a

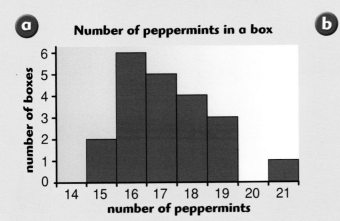

Number of peppermints in a box

b **Height to the nearest 10 cm of children in my class**

Height in cm	110	120	130	140	150
No of children	1	16	9	2	1

c

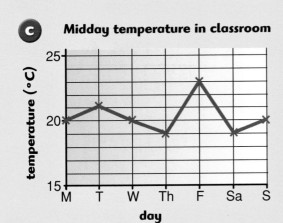

Midday temperature in classroom

d **Score when 2 dice are rolled 30 times**

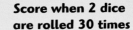
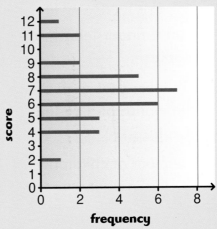

Let's investigate Work with a partner.

3 Draw a graph to represent imaginary data about shoe sizes.
The mode must be 4 and the range must be 10.

You need

squared paper

Let's practise

1 Write the median of each set of data.

a 146 cm   132 cm   128 cm   140 cm   128 cm

b 15   30   4   17   12

c $\frac{1}{4}$ $\frac{1}{8}$ $\frac{1}{5}$ $\frac{1}{7}$ $\frac{1}{12}$

d 70 kg   73 kg   81 kg   68 kg   71 kg

e 98   113   106

f 1 l   2·5 l   0·5 l   4 l   3·5 l

g £2·75   £8·50   £3·06   £5·61   £5·40

h 600   400   1200   300   800   1500   100

Let's solve problems

2 What is the median of all the prime numbers less than 100?

Let's investigate

3 Investigate the median for each of the following groups.

a The number of letters in the full names of 5 people in your class.

b The total finger-length of 3 people.

c The number that gives the day of the month of 9 people's birthdays.

d The number of children in each class in your school.